Pierre Marie François Pagès

Travels Round the World

In the years 1767, 1768, 1769, 1770, 1771. Vol. 2

Pierre Marie François Pagès

Travels Round the World
In the years 1767, 1768, 1769, 1770, 1771. Vol. 2

ISBN/EAN: 9783337344443

Printed in Europe, USA, Canada, Australia, Japan

Cover: Foto ©Andreas Hilbeck / pixelio.de

More available books at **www.hansebooks.com**

TRAVELS
ROUND THE WORLD,

IN THE YEARS

1767, 1768, 1769, 1770, 1771,

BY

MONSIEUR DE PAGÉS;

CAPTAIN IN THE FRENCH NAVY, KNIGHT OF THE
ROYAL AND MILITARY ORDER OF ST. LOUIS,
AND CORRESPONDING MEMBER OF THE
ACADEMY OF SCIENCES
AT PARIS.

TRANSLATED FROM THE FRENCH.

THE SECOND EDITION,
CORRECTED AND ENLARGED.

VOLUME THE SECOND.

LONDON:
PRINTED FOR J. MURRAY, N° 32, FLEET STREET.
M.DCC.XCIII.

CONTENTS.

VOLUME II.

PART II.

CHAP. I.

DEPARTURE from Batavia.—Meteorological observations made in different latitudes where the winds are regulated by the seasons, and inferences drawn from them.—Nautical description of the island of Bombay.—Anchorage on the coast of this island - - Page 1

CHAP. II.

Description of the city and island of Bombay.—The Author takes a passage from thence to Surat.—The harbour and city of Surat described.—Particulars relative to the different tribes of Gentoo Indians - 12

CHAP. III.

The Author quits Surat, and, assuming the dress of an Indian, penetrates into the country of the Marattas.—Customs of the natives.—Their remarkable delicacy.—Arrival at the district of Damum.—Rites and ceremonies of the inhabitants.—Reflections on the religious worship of the Bramins - 21

CHAP. IV.

Description of the country betwixt Trapore and Agassan, in the Maratta dominions. —Its cultivation, natural productions, and animals.—The houses and dress of the inhabitants described.—Their rites of interment.—Police and government of the Marratta provinces.—The Author reaches the island of Salset - - 30

CHAP. V.

Comparison, in point of morals, between the natives of the Maratta provinces, and the European and Persian settlers.—Simplicity and mildness of the Bramins in their government of the Gentoo tribes.—The Author

Author reasons upon the gentle manners and disposition of the natives of India, for which he endeavours to account.—He describes his own mode of life during his stay on the island of Samar - - 41

CHAP. VI.

Probity and hospitality of the Gentoos.— Their carnival described. — The Author arrives at Surat.—Its situation, extensive commerce, and flourishing state of the inhabitants.—Splendid stile of living of a private merchant.—Magnificent display of the Nabob on a public occasion - 52

CHAP. VII.

The Author leaves Surat, and arrives by sea at Mascate in Arabia Felix.—Sound policy of the Iman or sovereign of this kingdom.—Departure from Mascate for the Persian Gulf.—Singular custom of the Indian mariners in the Straits of Ormus 60

CHAP. VIII.

Character of the Dervises and Moorish Musfulmen of Asia.—The opinion the Asiatics in general entertain of Europeans.—Singular mathematical demonstration of the Indian philosophers.—The Author arrives at Bender Abouchier, in Persia - 70

CHAP. IX.

Anchorage on the coast of the island of Careith.—Passage from thence to the mouth of the Euphrates.—Description of this river and the Curd Coast.—Arrival at Bassora - - - - 78

CHAP. X.

Description of the city of Bassora.—Politic conduct of the English in obtaining a footing there.—The Author quits Bassora to join a caravan of Arabian shepherds for Aleppo - - - - 85

CHAP. XI.

The Author sets out with the caravan on his journey through the Desert.—An Arabian encampment is discovered.—Curious ceremonies at meeting, betwixt the Arabs and the Bedouin shepherds.—The Author visits the Arabian camp, and describes the pursuits and mode of life of the Arabs - 92

CHAP,

CHAP. XII.

Expedients the Arab employs to shelter himself, in the desert, from the scorching winds and reflection of the sands.—Character of the Arabs.—Their police, and civil regulations.—Political considerations upon the right of the wandering Arab to the desert he inhabits - - 101

CHAP. XIII.

Contrast betwixt the simple Arab, and the inhabitant of a refined country.—Amusements and employments of the natives of the desert.—The march of a tribe of Arabs across the desert described.—The caravan of shepherds resumes its journey.—And the Author describes a very picturesque scene in the desert. - - 112

CHAP. XIV.

The Author's companions make an unprovoked attack upon a few Arabs—they are surprized, in consequence, by a large body of Arabian horse and foot.—Several skirmishes ensue, in which the caravan is worsted by

the

the Arabs.—The Author, in his subsequent flight, suffers almost inexpressible hardships, and loses his baggage, his money, and his provisions - - - 122

CHAP. XV.

The Author and his companions escape from the Arabs their pursuers.—Friendly attentions of the Bedouin shepherds.—A fresh alarm renews the Author's sufferings.—Description of the Arabian dromedary 135

CHAP. XVI.

The company reach several high mountains, which announce their being on the border of the desert.—After various alarms and difficulties, they at length meet with a village, situated in a cultivated country - 142

CHAP. XVII.

The scene improves upon the Author and his companions, who are agreeably surprized at finding themselves freed from any further molestation from the Arabs.—They enter Turkey, and after passing several populous villages, reach Damascus - 151

CHAP.

CHAP. XVIII.

The Author quits Damascus, and passes through a mountainous but fertile country.—Hospitality and excellent character of the mountaineers.—Arrival at Baruth, and departure thence for Quesrouan.—The Author visits several convents, and arrives at the hospice of Aintoura - - 159

CHAP. XIX.

Description of the hospice of Aintoura, and the mountain on which it is situated.—The author proceeds to Jelton, and visits the Cheik or lord of the country.—His stay at the house of this Cheik, and the visits he pays to several others.—Description of the village of Jelton.—Police, customs, and religious rites of the inhabitants of the province of Quesrouan - - 168

CHAP. XX.

The Author quits Jelton, and makes excursions among the high mountains.—He arrives at the village of Mafra, and is hospitably received by a priest.—Rural mode of life of the inhabitants - 180

CHAP. XXI.

Arrival at a fertile plain, on which several ancient ruins are discovered.—Description of a temple of great antiquity, and other interesting monuments.—The Author reaches the villages of Besommar and Agousta, where he is kindly received by the ecclesiastics - - - - 187

CHAP. XXII.

The Author concludes his romantic excursion, and returns to Baruth.—He repairs from thence to Sidon, with a view to obtain a passage to France, but is disappointed.— He makes a considerable stay at Sidon, at the house of the French consul.—The antiquities in Sidon and its environs described.— Habits and sentiments of the natives of the mountains - - - 199

CHAP. XXIII.

Observations on the fine climate and productions of the southern parts of Syria.— Simple and industrious character of the inhabitants, contrasted with the luxury of Europe.

Europe.—The monks of Syria described. —Reflections on celibacy and matrimony 208

CHAP. XXIV.

Singular opinions of the Asiatics respecting the sexes, and the commerce which should be maintained betwixt them.—Abject state of the females in the nations of the east.— Diversions and pursuits of the Syrian women.—Tenacity of the natives of Syria in preserving their ancient customs.—Their social distinctions - - 218

CHAP. XXV.

The Author returns to the Syrian Mountains. —The village of Abey and its environs described.—Ceremonies observed at a Drusan funeral.—Pastoral mode of life of the Druses.—Residence in the town of Dair-el-Kamar - - - 232

CHAP. XXVI.

Government and political regulations of the Land of Souf.—Sagacity of the grand emir of Turkey in dividing the interests of the cheiks

cheiks or governors.—State of warfare betwixt the different tribes.—Their inveterate hatred to strangers.—Regulations of internal policy - - 241

CHAP. XXVII.

Various particulars respecting the customs and religious tenets of the inhabitants of the land of Souf.—The Author returns to Baruth, and afterwards visits Mafra and several other villages in the province of Quesrouan. Comparison betwixt the manners and principles of the Greeks and Arabs - 249

CHAP. XXVIII.

The Author embarks at St. Jean d'Acre for Marseilles.—The vessel touches at Limba, a Turkish port, where she is in danger of being detained.—The contempt in which the French, and other European merchants, in the Turkish ports, are held by the Turks, accounted for.—After touching at Tunis, the Author at length reaches Maseilles 258

TRAVELS
ROUND THE WORLD,
BY SEA AND LAND.

PART II.

CHAP. I.

Departure from Batavia—Meteorological observations made in different latitudes where the winds are regulated by the seasons, and inferences drawn from them—nautical description of the island of Bombay—anchorage on the coast of this island.

WE sailed for Bombay and Surat on the 2d of August 1769, left Milles isles on the starboard, and Honduras with its adjacent islands on our larboard; and at the approach of night found we had cleared their several rocks. In the course of the night we doubled Bantam, and entered the streights of the Sound, and upon the return of day had left Towards-Peper considerably astern of us. Having ſtood ſouthward, in order to paſs between Prince's Iſland and the coaſt of Java, where we took in freſh water, we ſhaped our courſe W. and S. W. till we reached the latitude of twelve degrees; and then ſtood W. The wind, which had continued invariably in the S. and S. S. W. as we approached the meridian of the Maldive iſlands, ſhifted to the E. and E. S. E.

Having paſſed between the iſlands of Amarante, which we could not diſtinguiſh, we ſtood W. N. W. then N. W.; and, reaching the latitude of ſix degrees, under the meridian of the iſland of Bourbon, ſteered towards the north. The wind had blown conſtantly from the E. and E. S. E. but here it began to die away, and continued very moderate till we reached the ſeventh degree of northern latitude, where we had for ſeveral days calms and ſtorms alternately; after which the wind ſhifted to the weſt.

Having been in exactly ſimilar climates previouſly to my arrival in the Philippine iſles, I was now, for the ſecond time, in thoſe regions

regions at sea where the winds are regulated by the seasons; and therefore shall take the liberty to make a few observations on this subject.

In the first place, I observed in the ocean, as well as in the South and Indian seas, that the wind blew, without any variation, from the east when we were near the tropics; but that it varied from the direct point towards the north or south, according to the precise latitude of the ship. I have likewise observed in all countries whatever, that when the sky is serene the east or easterly winds are much more frequent than those of the west; that a north-west wind in a northern, and south-west in a southern latitude, are the attendants of fine weather; but that the wind no sooner shifts into the north-west under a southern, or into the south-west under a northern latitude, than we are with equal probability to expect rain. That with a south-east wind in a northern, and north-east in a southern latitude, we may generally expect rain; while the north-east north, and south-east south of the line, are the ordinary forerunners of fair weather.

B 2   I ob-

I observed in America, at the Philippine isles, and I know the same thing happens on the coast of India, whither I am bound, that during the rainy season the wind blows constantly from the quarter of the west. This season sets in at all places between the tropics and the line, upon the sun's approaching the zenith of their respective climates. Thus the sun having crossed the equator in his progress northward, the rains begin to fall in all regions visited by his vertical rays; while the corresponding parts of the globe south of the line enter into their dry season. And in the same manner when those southern climates have their rain, the northern enjoy their fair weather. This regular course, however, observed by the rain and west winds, only extends to coasts and mainlands, or to seas, which, from their contiguity to these, share in all the accidents attendant upon their nature and situation.

Between the tropics the east or trade winds blow all round the globe with no other interruption than what is occasioned by by vapours exhaled by the fun's rays, when he approaches the zenith of a particular climate; and then the wind fhifts its direction from eaft to weft. In the Eaft Indies thefe winds are known by the name of monfoons; in the Antilles and Ifle of France, by that of hivernage; and on the coafts of America, Africa, China, and in the interior parts of the Arabian and Perfian feas, by that of the rainy feafon. In fhort, I have obferved, that commonly in all high latitudes continued rains are accompanied with wefterly winds.

The wind being now decidedly in the weft, we ftood N. N. E. and afterwards N. E. till we came to the latitude of fourteen degrees. Here we kept the cap in the E. N. E. with the wind in the N. W.; and as we imagined we were approaching the found, we hove the lead; and found feventy fathoms water on a fandy bottom. Having fhaped our courfe towards the eaft, we quickly difcovered land, which we found to be the mountains of Baffein, and foon came in view of Carangear and the ifle of Bombay; and as we had thirty fathoms water we ftood directly for the point of Malabar. Night came on, and we continued to purfue the fame courfe till eleven, when the water fhallowing to twelve fathoms, with the wind at N. W. we kept as clofe as poffible to the W. S. W. We ftood in this dangerous direction till near five in the morning, which, to thofe who are acquainted with our precife fituation, will appear a great deal too long. Having been carried by a rapid current greatly towards the fouth, at break of day we found ourfelves immediately under *Chaoul*. This is a round hill fituated on the mainland, bearing fouth from the entrance of Bombay; and confequently we had fallen confiderably to leeward. We attempted to recover the advantage we had loft by tacking; but the wind, which blew conftantly from the N. W. and W. N. W. having frefhened, we were driven about for the fpace of two days. Finding we had provifions only for three more, it was propofed to put into a fort of harbour named Rajapour, fituated in a bay of the mainland; but befides that it might be particularly critical at prefent, as

the

the period of the weft winds was drawing to a clofe, we knew very little of the accommodation it afforded to fhipping. It was therefore propofed that we fhould proceed and lay in provifions at Goa; but as the weft wind ftill prevailed, it was found that if we embraced this refolution we fhould be under the neceffity of crofling the line once more, in order to fall in with a wind favourable for Bombay; a circumftance which would tend greatly to protract our voyage. In the mean time the wind fhifted to the fouth-weft, and blew very frefh; when directing our courfe a little towards the north, in five days it became calm, and the wind fhifting from the S. E. to the W. N. W. we again came in view of Chaoul and Carangear: and in a fhort time faw the light-houfe and white rounds of Old Women Ifland. Thefe white rounds are buildings erected with arcades, in a circular form, for the purpofe of beacons, and appear like fo many large pigeon-houfes which have been lately white-wafhed. They ftand on a low ftrip of land, which ftretches fouth from the ifle of Bombay, and is known by the name of

Old

Old Women Island. On the island of Bombay are beacons of a similar kind; whilst one of the city churches, and the little town of Maheim, are also employed as guides to the mariner. Maheim lies N. W. of the island, and varies in its appearance by reason of some very tall trees, which serve to point it out to our notice.

At the distance of three leagues south-west from the island of Bombay, we had fifteen fathoms water; and having taken a pilot on board, we sailed eastward, in order to double a reef of rocks at the point of Old Women Island, which stretch in two branches south-east and south-west a league into the sea. In passing these rocks we kept at a league and a half's distance from the shore, but then veered round, putting the cap in the N. E. and afterwards in the N. N. E. being at the same time extremely careful not to approach the coast of Bombay nearer than seven fathoms water. We left on our right the rocks *Sunquen* and *Droven*, both of them being within the point at the light-house of Old Women Island. That of Sunquen is the outermost and farthest theft advanced into the fea, and confequently the moft dangerous to navigation; it lies in a direct line with the north baftion of the fort, and a houfe named Maffagon. This building is kept in repair, and white-wafhed from time to time, for the purpofe of a beacon; and may be diftinguifhed by its fquare form, and its being fituated on an eminence N. E. from the city of Bombay. The rock Droven is near the land, and in the direction of a wood of cocoa-trees on Old Women Ifland, and a tall cocoa-trunk N. W. from the fort. This wood of cocoa-trees fhould be made to open a little in the weft, I mean to fhift their pofition a little weft of the above-mentioned cocoa-trunk, which is kept ftanding for this purpofe alone. It was impoffible for us to difcover this rock without failing too near the fhore; and therefore fteering N. and N. and a quarter E. we left a little ifland named Crofs on our left, at a very fmall diftance. As foon as we got into the road, we coafted the ifland of Bombay at the diftance of a ftone's caft from the beach. I have only one further obfervation, in the way of caution

tion to the pilot in approaching this shore, and that is, to be on his guard against another rock, called Middle-Ground, which is situated E. and a quarter S. E. at the distance of a short league from the church of Bombay. The ships come to anchor between this rock and the shore, close to the town, which they may approach to a distance within the reach of the voice, with perfect safety.

Old Women Island is separated from the isle of Bombay only by a reef of rocks, which are never wholly under water, except during high tides; and even then, though the island is on a level with the surface of the water, still it is extremely difficult of access, from the dangerous rocks with which it is surrounded. The communication between Old Women Island and Bombay lies entirely under the eye of a battery. We now observed the glacis of the city, whose walls border on the sea, and at the same time a couple of batteries placed in the front of the glacis. The top of the ditch, besides being under a bastion, is secured by a work more particularly intended for its defence. The
cannon

cannon of this baftion and its curtine, as well as thofe of the oppofite baftion, with a double battery, by which the former are flanked, are all meant for the protection of the bay.

There is a creek occafionally ufed as a harbour, on the confines of which ftand an arfenal, dry docks, and houfes for the accommodation of the company's fervants. The city wall, interrupted by the principal harbour, re-appears at this little creek, and extends all the way to a fort which was erected by the Portuguefe. This city, though well fortified on the fide of the fea, is in but an indifferent ftate of defence towards the land, being only inclofed by a plain wall mounted with a number of pitiful little baftions. It is furrounded however by a very deep ditch, and a glacis, kept in excellent repair, befides which feveral of the gates have the additional advantage of half-moons. There is in its vicinity an eminence named Hongary, which appears to me to be of the greateft importance to the fecurity of Bombay.

CHAP. II.

Description of the city and island of Bombay.—The Author takes a passage from thence to Surat.—The harbour and city of Surat described.—Particulars relative to the different tribes of Gentoo Indians.

THE city of Bombay, though populous, and containing a number of handsome houses, is for the greatest part ill built and irregular. The principal suburbs are Hongary and Palmeyra, the last of which is crouded with Indians, and by far the most pleasant.

The island is in general extremely narrow, not exceeding in some places half a league; but spreads out to a considerable extent in the quarter of Maheim. It is extremely steep, surrounded with rocks consisting of gravel combined with a little earth, and is every where difficult of access, not excepting even the bay, particularly at low water. The inland country, though

not

not very high, is for the moſt part of an uneven and rugged ſurface. But the excellent accommodation it affords to ſhipping, by which it is rendered the firſt harbour on the mainland of India, and not the advantages of its ſoil, was the great inducement to ſettle on this iſland. It is a ſtrong hold, of infinite importance to the Engliſh, and indeed may be conſidered as the baſis of that extenſive dominion they have found means to eſtabliſh in this part of the world.

The ſterility of its ſoil renders living at Bombay difficult and expenſive; the Engliſh, however, are ſupplied with proviſions by the Marrattas of Salſet, Baſſein, and other parts of the mainland. The late extenſion of the Engliſh boundaries in theſe regions has greatly enhanced the value, as well as added to the ſecurity, of this ſettlement.

The veſſel on board which I took my paſſage from Batavia having now accompliſhed her buſineſs at this port, I reſolved to take a paſſage in her to Surat; and accordingly we weighed, and got under ſail the 25th of September. The wind blowing

ing almoſt fair into the mouth of the harbour, we were obliged to tack; and on this occaſion two reefs of rocks, which extend confiderably into the fea, and which are named Carangear's Feet, and the Rock of Chaoul, from fome hills in their vicinity, gave us much uneafineſs. Chaoul is a large high hill, nearly of a circular form, and is fituated on the mainland fouth from Bombay. Carangear is likewife a pretty high hill, ſtanding on a little iſland nearer the mainland than that of Bombay. It rifes in the form of two pyramidal fections, which prefent an eliptic curve, and are diſtinguifhed from each other by the Great and Little Carangear.

Having doubled the rocky points of Old Women Ifland, we fhaped a N. N. W. courfe, in twelve fathoms water. The land breeze, which came from the S. E. was very inconfiderable, while that from the N. W. and confequently againſt us, was much more powerful. But at length, after being carried greatly towards the fouth, and much retarded by currents, tides, and winds, we came, on the eighth day, in view

of

of Cape St. John, which forms the entrance to the gulph of Cambaia. The fituation of this gulph may be afcertained by the peak of St. John, which is a little diftance fouth of it, and is formed by a part of a mountain, in the fhape of a needle, detached from the main body. Next day we doubled the cape, but at the diftance of four leagues, in order to avoid the rocks in its vicinity.

We kept in foundings of from fifteen to eighteen fathoms water, carefully avoiding thofe of twelve on the fide of the main, as they border on a reef of dangerous rocks, which ftretch up the middle of the gulph. We fteered acrofs a curvature, formed by a fweep of the Marratta and Damum coafts, and on the 6th of September faw the fhipping which lay at anchor in the harbour of Surat. Next day we entered the road, and came to moorings in ten fathoms water, on a bottom of clay. This is a very large and beautiful road, but expofed to every wind, and at too great a diftance from the land.

In

In the prefent feafon, the fea runs with much lefs violence than either at Bombay or in the gulph; but during the rainy months, befides the adjacent grounds being completely overflowed, it is impoffible to lie at anchor in the road, on account of a ftrong current, the inundations of the river, and the very high winds that fet in from the ocean. The moft convenient ftation for fhipping is at a village fituated on the right fide, and about the diftance of a league from the point of the firft bank of the river. The city of Surat ftands on the left, about five leagues from the mouth of the river. In the dry feafon it is only navigable fo high up to fmall veffels of three hundred tons; but in the rainy months the largeft fhips in the road fail up and winter at Surat. As foon as we dropped anchor I fet out for the capital. The caftle, which ftands on the border of the river, and within the bounds of the city, was the firft object of my attention; a piece of fortification, which, though irregular, and executed in a ftyle very different from the European tafte,

is

is not without merit. It confifts of a number of femicircular towers, mutually flanking each other, and commanding the city and river. The adjacent grounds, to a confiderable extent, are free from all incumbrances; but the main building, originally well conftructed, is very old, and in want of many repairs, efpecially on the fide of the river. The Britifh and Moorifh flags are equally difplayed from a baftion of the caftle; but, though the Englifh troops have only poffeffion of fome of the gates and a fingle baftion, all real authority both in town and country is known to refide in them. The remaining gates are occupied by the forces of the Nabob, who, however, like all other Indian princes in their alliance, is allowed the exercife of his prerogatives only in matters of little moment.

Two gates in the exterior wall (for properly Surat confifts of two cities, the one erected in the bofom of the other) are in the hands of the Marrattas of Guzurat, who receive a kind of tribute from the inhabitants, when they are in a condition to exact it by force.

Vol. II.　　　　C　　　　The

The prodigious extent of this city, its vaft population, the immenfe wealth of fome, and the affluent or eafy condition of the people in general, the numerous carriages, a moft extenfive commerce, the many beautiful houfes in the Moorifh tafte, the cheapnefs and abundance of all the neceffaries of life; every object, in fhort, within the walls of Surat, tends to imprefs the mind of a ftranger with ideas of its great refources and importance.

During my fhort refidence here, the Nabob made his appearance in public. His highnefs was efcorted by three thoufand regular troops, befides an equal number of men on foot, on horfeback, or in palanquins; a proceffion well calculated to give fome idea of Afiatic pomp and magnificence. In his train was a band of mufic, remarkable only for its noife, together with a number of camels, and four elephants richly caparifoned.

But what I admired moft is the induftrious character of both fexes among the Gentoo Indians. Befides a few of the Banians, who attach themfelves to commerce,
the

the Gentoos of the inferior cafts perform all the drudgery and fevere labour of the country. Some of thefe cafts, I underftand, are believers in the ancient Metempfychofis.

There is here a race of people named Perfians, or Guebres, who ftill retain fome remains of the law of Zoroafter, and who adore the Divinity under the fymbol of fire. They are eminently diftinguifhed by their works of charity, having erected hofpitals for the accommodation of the fick and difeafed, as well as for feeding the deftitute of the inferior animals.

Many things are related of the Yoguis, or penitential Gentoos, which may feem fomewhat incredible. There are fome among them, I was affured, who pafs their lives with one arm ftretched in the air; others, without ever treading the ground, make the tour of a kingdom by crawling on their bellies; while a third fort remain pinned to the fpot whereon they have been accidentally placed, and, were no charitably difpofed perfon to interpofe and draw them afide, rather than quit their

poft

post they would suffer themselves to be crushed to death by whatever happened to be passing on the road.

One day I met with one of those Yoguis preaching near a pagoda, on the border of a lake, and at the same time doing penance, but of a nature which a sense of decency forbids me to mention. The whim of the moment induced him to follow me during my excursion, nor was it by any means in my power to get rid of him before we returned to the border of the lake where I had found him. The penitential Gentoo is held in high veneration among the people, who refuse nothing he asks, and permit him to take, at his discretion, whatever he has occasion for. In the house of a Banian, whom I was going to wait upon, when I was followed by this Yoguis, he seized and carried off several small articles, without, apparently at least, giving the smallest offence.

All the inhabitants of the first distinction in Surat, and at least one half of those of inferior condition, are followers of Mahomet; next to them in number are the

Gentoos;

Gentoos; then the Perfians; while the Jews and Chriftians, the laft of whom do not exceed five hundred perfons, make the fmalleft clafs.

CHAP. III.

The Author quits Surat, and, affuming the drefs of an Indian, penetrates into the country of the Marrattas.—Cuftoms of the natives.—Their remarkable delicacy.—Arrival at the diftrict of Damum.—Rites and ceremonies of the inhabitants.—Reflections on the religious worfhip of the Bramins.

BEING extremely defirous to obtain fome knowledge of the Marratta tribes, I dreffed myfelf in the fafhion of that country; and, having obtained a guide from the fame nation, fix days after my arrival, departed from Surat. In a progrefs through the country, I paffed villages at regular ftages of four leagues, and fometimes at a fhorter diftance. In their vicinity

vicinity are crops of Indian corn, rice, vegetables, a fpecies of grain from which they extract oil, and another, the ftalks of which fupply them with materials for cordage. The country is much interfected with rivers, which however are very inconfiderable, except in the rainy feafon. After a journey of ten leagues, I came to a town called Naufary, of fmall extent, but containing a very confiderable cotton manufactory. It has a fort, which belongs to the Marrattas, and is furrounded with pagodas, gardens, and beautiful flower-plots. The unufual familiarity, common in this country, among all the different tribes of animals, which fported before us with the moft carelefs indifference, is not a little furprifing to a ftranger. The birds, undifmayed by our approach, perched upon the trees and fwarmed among the branches, as if they conceived man to be of a nature equally quiet and inoffenfive with themfelves; while the monkey and fquirrel climbed the wall, gamboled on the houfetop, and leapt with confidence and alacrity from one bough to another over our heads.

Even

Even the more formidable quadrupeds seem to have lost their natural ferocity in the same harmless dispositions; and hence the apprehensions commonly occasioned by the proximity of such neighbours, no longer disquiet the minds of the natives. Happy effect of those mild and innocent manners, whence have arisen peace and protection to all the inferior animals!

The inhabitants are divided into different casts, the lowest of which are permitted by their rules to eat flesh on particular occasions; those of an intermediate order eat fish, fruit, and vegetables only; while the Banian and Bramin, who belong to the highest cast, live on nothing but the produce of the soil, in which however milk and butter are included. Finding myself much fatigued, upon my arrival at Naufary, for I had travelled on foot, I hired an ox, the only animal used for the saddle in this country, and continued my travels to Gondivy. I sat down to dine, but was a good deal surprised to observe leaves placed on the table instead of plates, which, upon finishing my meal, I was obliged to throw away with my own hands. I was at the fame time prefented with a leaf-goblet, which, after having ufed, was difpofed of in like manner. It is faid that a ftrict Gentoo would rather fubmit to martyrdom than defile the purity of his perfon, by coming in contact with that part of the cup which has been at the mouth of a man of a different caft. The Moor, the Gentoo, the Perfian, and Chriftian, all obferve the fame extreme delicacy in regard to each other. In the town of Gondivy, a confiderable part of the inhabitants are Perfians, and of the fame fect with thofe I faw at Surat. The Perfians, or Guebres as they are fometimes called, are a people defcended from the ancient inhabitants of Perfia, who, upon being expatriated by their conqueror on account of their religion, migrated hither, and their pofterity are now fcattered all over this country.

Having proceeded eight leagues further, through a country fit only for pafture, and in many places in the moft defolate ftate, I arrived at Gondivy in Pardy, a fmall town, which forms the domains of a little fovereign

reign prince. Next day I reached De-
mum or Damum; but, as I had no inclination to see the governor, whom I ought
to have waited upon, I went on without
stopping, and slept at a quarter of a league
distance, in a little town composed of Gentoos and a few Christians. They are subject
to the Portuguese, who possess a small territory, and about four leagues of this coast,
comprehending five or six villages, on a
dry and inhospitable soil. These people
are so poor and necessitous, that I have
seen Christians themselves obliged, for subsistence, to work as labourers to the Marrattas; a state of indigence, however,
which has hitherto been unable either to
subdue their arrogance or stimulate their
industry. Thus far on my way from Surat,
I had not met with a single Christian; here,
however, I discovered my host to be a man
of the same religious persuasion with myself.
In the course of the next day, I passed
very handsome villages belonging to the
Marrattas of Narguoil and Barauly; and
the day following, after being a week upon
the road, I arrived at the village of Danou,

the

the minifter of which, an Indian Portuguefe, I made it my bufinefs to wait upon.

This diftrict of Damum was formerly conquered and poffefied by the Portuguefe, and only paffed within thefe thirty years to the Marrattas; who having granted toleration to all religious fects, the Chriftians have become frequent in every part of the country. In this village is a church, a paftor, and a very confiderable body of Chriftians. I was invited to a marriage in the neighbourhood, at which the Marrattas, and even the Bramins, who were led by curiofity to attend this feftival, fome at the ceremony of the church, others at the fubfequent diverfions, conducted themfelves with fuch decency of behaviour, as in fimilar fituations we but rarely meet with among Chriftians, particularly where they find themfelves lords of the country. Religious proceffions, the ceremony of burial, the ufe of the crofs on the highways, and in general all the rites of Chriftian worfhip, are exercifed here with equal freedom as in the kingdom of France.

The appearance of the Marrattas, of both fexes, particularly the women, confirms

firms me in an opinion I had early formed of their active and induftrious difpofition. There are, however, among the natives fome who affect to be Portuguefe, but who in fact are Gentoo Chriftians, and feem to have attached themfelves to the religion and fociety of the Portuguefe from no other motive than that of having it more eafily in their power to pafs their lives in vanity and idlenefs; an abufe, however, probably proceeding from that miferable example of the Chriftian life, which the convicts of the parent country, whom it has been ufual to tranfport hither for their crimes, offer to the imitation of the natives. The Gentoos are fociable, humane, and hofpitable; and, during my refidence in their country, I never had occafion to obferve a fingle inftance of violence or difpute. They rear numerous herds of cattle; but fuch is their veneration for thefe animals, on account of their ufeful and patient fervices to man, that to kill or even maim one of them is deemed a capital offence.

Among the innumerable idols which fill their pagodas, I faw various kinds of beafts, trees, and even ftones. The moft grotefque

and

and extravagant of thefe figures are emblematical reprefentations of the Divinity; while their other idols, of every denomination, are of inferior order, and only intitled to adoration as they are the reprefentatives and monitors of particular favours they have received, from time to time, from the beneficence of the Deity. Like the Perfians and Muffulmen, they make frequent ufe of water for the purification of their bodies; but of fuch only as is contained in particular lakes; I faw one of thefe between Baffan and Agaffan, on the borders of which ftand a number of very fine pagodas. I was affured by a Bramin, with whom I had the pleafure to make an acquaintance in my peregrinations through this country, that he worfhipped one God only; who, after having cleared the world of giants and malefactors, had afcended into heaven. I am far from being inclined to charge this people with idolatry in the vulgar and literal fenfe of that word; indeed in ftrict language I can fcarcely fuppofe there is one real idolater on the face of the earth; for, although the Divine effence is often adored under fome material form by which he is

meant

meant to be reprefented, ftill I am perfuaded there is no race of men, how barbarous foever, who worfhip an idol on its own account; and diftinct from its great original. I once entered into converfation with a Bramin, in a Chriftian church, while the prieft was adminiftering the facrament of baptifm, and was at pains to explain to him the duties and obligations which I conceived to be implied in that rite. Having liftened with attention, he feemed much pleafed with the lame account I was able to give of them, and concluded his reply by obferving, that the great objects of both our religions appeared to him to be the fame.

During the fhort time I paffed in this village, a little fleet of their fhips of war, about the fize of our tartans, entered the river. They are called *Galvettes*, and built to carry four and fometimes fix guns. Their chief employment is to fcour the coafts of a race of pirates named *Chamchas*, who fally from the bottom of the gulph of Guzurat, and commit depredations upon fuch trading veffels as they happen to furprife in thofe feas.

CHAP.

CHAP. IV.

Description of the country betwixt Trapore and Agaſſan, in the Marratta dominions. —Its cultivation, natural productions, and animals.—The houſes and dreſs of the inhabitants deſcribed.—Their rites of interment.—Police and government of the Marratta provinces.—The author reaches the iſland of Salſet.

ON the 12th of November, having reſumed my journey, I paſſed Trapore, a city of ſome extent, populous, and defended by a fort. My next ſtage was Maheim, a large town, inhabited chiefly by Bramins; and the day following I came to Agaſſan, where I lived with a Frenchman, who had the command of thirty Europeans, in the ſervice of a Rajah or Marratta prince, at Barauda, in the province of Guzurat. The Rajah of this province reſides at *Puna*, or Poney, a large city, ſituated in the interior parts of the country, and is one of the moſt powerful of theſe princes.

Agaſſan

Agaſſan ſtands at the diſtance of five leagues from another confiderable town, named Baſſan, which, having the advantages of a good road and excellent river, fits out ſhips for the purpoſe of trading along the coaſt of Arabia. The ſea-coaſt is very ſtrongly fortified, while the country from Trapore is extremely populous, and enlivened with frequent and beautiful gardens. Befides herbs and vegetables, the inhabitants cultivate the fugar-cane, cocoa, and fig-trees. From Baſſan to Agaſſan, the traveller fcarce meets with an acre of waſte or fallow-ground. The rich verdure and vegetation of their gardens are, however, in a great degree, owing to the common ufe of wheel-wells, which are made to water the foil, by means of buffaloes; but in the more central diſtricts, and even along the coaſt from Trapore to Pardy, the foil is in general extremely dry during the fix months of fair weather. On the contrary, it is wholly under water in the rainy feafon, when there fprings up an amazing quantity of grafs, which, as the ground is either too moiſt or too dry to give birth to a fingle ſhrub, gives the face of the

country

country the appearance of one continued meadow. The moſt common tree, in the environs of Surat, is the wild date, as is a ſpecies of wild palm in the more inland country. The chief advantage the natives derive from theſe trees conſiſts in their ſap, which they are accuſtomed either to drink in its natural ſtate, or to manufacture into a kind of brandy. The wood and leaves are likewiſe of uſe in the conſtruction of houſes. Indian corn is the prevailing crop in the quarter of Surat, and rice in the parts which are ſituated more to the ſouth. The natives diſcover ſkill as well as induſtry in the cultivation of their farms. As ſoon as the annual floods have withdrawn, the graſs, which has in that interval grown up, having been collected in heaps, is burned, and the aſhes are employed as manure for the purpoſe of enriching their rice fields. The crops of rice and corn are raiſed by very different methods. The Indian farmer, having ſowed his rice in ground prepared and manured for the purpoſe, at a certain period tranſplants it into a new field, where it remains till it comes to maturity, and is cut down.

The

The extreme scarcity of water, which prevails here constantly for the space of six months in the year, serves to exercise the humanity and beneficence of many pious and well-disposed persons. Hence those deep wells, which have been dug and constructed at a great expence, with the convenience of stairs reaching to the edge of the water; while a fund is allotted for the purposes of affording them occasional repairs, of maintaining a number of watermen, and of furnishing such utensils as are necessary for drawing water and giving drink to the cattle.

In other places it has been found expedient to construct large and capacious ponds, which serve to collect water during the rains, and to preserve it for public use in the course of the dry season. Such are the dimensions of many of these vast reservoirs, that the water is neither unwholesome nor unpalatable; and is in a particular manner the resource of the natives who live at a distance from rivers.

The most common animals in this country are tigers, monkies, and wild dogs, which

which are smaller in size than those of America. Of the feathered tribes, I saw the turtle-dove, some peacocks, numbers of parroquets, one or two species of small birds, and crows, in vast flocks, so tame that they used to attack our dishes upon the table. The other native animals of eastern countries descend but seldom from the mountains, preferring, under the shelter of their woods, a cooler and freer air than is to be found in the plain.

The houses in the country are but simple cottages, in some places constructed with bamboo, in others with the palm-tree, and thatched with leaves or hay. The wall consists of wattled work of osiers and bull-rushes plaistered over with mud. The town houses, however, are extremely different, many of them having a noble effect. In general they have two stories only; but each floor consists, if I may use the expression, of three amphitheatrical gradations, upon the highest of which, and in the opposite corners, are two apartments, intended to contain the most valuable family effects. The front of the build-

ing

ing is fupported on the infide by a certain number of pillars, and is open to the day; whilft the outer wall is furrounded by a kind of gallery, which embraces the other three fides of the houfe. The area of the firft gradation is laid with fine tapeftry, and here the family is accuftomed to receive and entertain their friends; it fupports likewife a large bafon, which is filled with water by means of a wheel-well, the machinery of which is erected in the firft ftory. The buffalo employed to work the machine turns the pivot, which is over his head, in his progrefs round the circumference of the well. The floor is paved with a certain compofition, confifting of a foft ftone pounded and mixed with a fpecies of plaifter made of oil and the whites of eggs. This cement, when properly prepared, becoming extremely folid and compact, acquires the appearance of a fmooth ftone of a fine varnifh, and has a more beautiful effect than that of our beft inlaid floors. On the top of the building is a flat roof or terrace, coated with the fame cement, which they name *algamaffe*.

The dreſs of the women is compoſed of a very long piece of painted callicoe, one half of which, after paſſing ſeveral times round the waiſt, is folded back and faſtened behind; the other half is thrown over the head, and falling down before, covers the arms and boſom, and is attached in folds to the girdle. In this manner one ſimple garment embraces the whole body, and even ſerves for a veil to the face. In the country, however, they frequently gather together what covers the head, and let it fall upon the ſhoulders, leaving the neck and boſom almoſt entirely expoſed, and on theſe occaſions, as it conſiſts of a very fine kind of cloth, it aſſumes the air of a ſaſh; but when at other times they chooſe to fold up the lower part of the robe, paſſing the end of it between the legs, it acquires the appearance of drawers, which deſcend to the middle of the thigh.

In town the men are uſually dreſſed in a long white robe, which has the appearance of a jacket ſewed to a kind of petticoat; but in the country they wear two long broad pieces of cloth, the one round their loins,

loins, the other over their shoulders, or perhaps only a sort of band passed between their thighs.

Rings seem to be a peculiar object of female ambition in every rank and condition of life, and are used to adorn the toes as well as the fingers. A bracelet of glass tied round the wrist, and one of silver round the ankle, are extremely common. Besides the ordinary ornaments of the ear, many wear a nose-jewel, or ring passed through the separation of the nostrils. On the forehead is sometimes a star punctured in the flesh; and the lower eye-lashes are often painted black, in order to enhance the brilliancy of the pupil.

The Gentoos sometimes inter, but more frequently burn the bodies of their dead; a rite usually performed on the bank of a river, over which they afterwards scatter the ashes of the deceased. A widow commonly mourns a year for the loss of her husband, and in this period devotes the first moments after she awakes in the morning to tears and lamentations.

There are still ladies, particularly in the higher casts, who insist upon their privilege of being burned upon the funeral piles of their husbands; but on such occasions it is the business of the assistants to suffocate the unhappy victim, by pouring pails of oil over her face, before she has been attacked by the flames. This religious attachment of the wife to the remains of her husband is nevertheless greatly on the decline.

On the 6th of December I proceeded by Bassan to the island of Salset, which is separated from the mainland by a branch of the sea, in some places extremely narrow, and only two leagues in breadth where I passed it. Salset is detached from the island of Bombay by another little arm of the sea, across which the English deserters easily swim in their way to the Marratta forts of Varsova and Bandora. Salset is eight leagues in breadth; and being covered with the mangoe, and other fruit-trees, which bear abundance of little fragrant blossoms, is much more pleasant than the mainland; but its gardens are few, and the soil not fertile.

I dwelt

I dwelt nearly in the centre of the ifland, at a town named Pary, and only at a fhort diftance from Malart. This laft place is the refidence of an Avaldor, deputy to the foubadar or governor of the province, who lives in a kind of fortrefs, called Tana, about five leagues diftant. Pary is in the vicinity of a fountain and two refervoirs, embellifhed by magnificent trees, and is placed in a moft agreeable and rural fituation. Here I made acquaintance with feveral Bramins, from whom I received in many inftances much kindnefs and civility.

The Marratta provinces are under the fupreme authority of Puna, but are adminiftered by governors, who delegate their power to commandants within their refpective jurifdictions. It is the duty of the Avaldor or commandant to collect the taxes, and in general to execute the orders of the foubadar, by means, if neceffary, of an armed force confifting of a body of fepoys.

Property in land is not transferrable as in Europe, but remains vefted exclufively in the fovereign, who farms it to the peafantry, and receives

receives a rent in kind, which has continued fixed from time immemorial at a certain proportion of the crop. This rent paid to the ſtate is extremely moderate; and in order to encourage the induſtry of the colomby, or farmer, who forms a caſt by himſelf, he is allowed certain chiefs, whoſe buſineſs it is to protect him in all the rights of his order. Other public burdens are very inconſiderable, not exceeding the annual ſum of five livres a family. As a particular encouragement to gardening, whatever portion of ground the farmer chooſes to employ in this manner he poſſeſſes rent-free for the ſpace of ten years, at the expiration of which period he pays to the *circar*, that is to the government, a third part of the produce. The ſoubadar is a kind of farmer general, who becomes bound to the ſovereign in a certain ſum for all the taxes of the province, and then collects them from the peaſantry in the beſt manner he can. The farmer, however, is in little danger of being oppreſſed, from the power and conſequence of his own chief, who is appointed by the ſtate expreſsly for his protection.

The public repairs of the province of every description, and the purveyance of the governor's household, are services performed by the people of whatever religion, and of either sex; for which, however, they receive a small gratuity.

CHAP. V.

Comparison, in point of morals, between the natives of the Marratta provinces, and the European and Persian settlers.—Simplicity and mildness of the Bramins in their government of the Gentoo tribes.—The Author reasons upon the gentle manners and disposition of the natives of India, for which he endeavours to account.—He describes his own mode of life during his stay on the island of Samar.

TOWARDS the end of January 1770, after making a considerable stay on this island, having learned that a ship belonging

longing to the French East India company, called The Indian, had anchored at Surat, I was defirous to embrace this opportunity of writing to my friends in Europe. Departing, therefore, from Salfet, I arrived in five days at Danou, whence it was eafy to have letters conveyed to the city of Surat; and as I returned by Baffan, I had a fecond opportunity of admiring the fimple but civilized and well-regulated manners of the natives. In the genius of the inhabitants, however, there are certain fhades of difference, chiefly arifing from the variety of religious opinions tolerated and exercifed in this country. The Portuguefe, as I have already obferved, are vain and indolent; the Mahometans, with all their fimplicity, are haughty, and ever prone to conceive themfelves of a condition fuperior to other men; the Perfians are an active and induftrious people, but extremely interefted; while the Gentoos, and above all the Bramins, are of unaffected fimple manners, gentle, regular, and temperate in the whole conduct of their lives. Although all public offices centre in the caft of the Bramins, they

they are peculiarly affable and condefcending; infomuch that I am fatisfied they are ftrangers to a phrafe fufficiently intelligible in the nations of Europe, I mean *the infolence of office*. The different chambers of adminiftration, as well as the courts of juftice, are open to the infpection of the public; while thofe who prefide over them are equally acceffible to the pooreft peafant as to men of the firft diftinction. Here the Soubadar exercifes all the functions of his office in perfon; and I have feen him, on different occafions, with no other veftment than a linen covering tied round his loins, feated with his legs acrofs on a carpet, writing on his knees, or liftening with great attention and humanity to the various fuits before him. It was difficult for me to affociate this aftonifhing fimplicity and benignity of character with the authority and importance of a fovereign; or to connect in my mind the notion of an extenfive population, a highly cultivated country, a numerous army, forts, garrifons, circumftances all expreffive of a large, civilized, and

and opulent kingdom, with the innocent and inoffenfive deportment of its rulers.

Upon my firft arrival at Salfet, the Deputy Soubadar, after receiving me in the beft manner, took occafion to obferve, that as Europeans were men of a fiery and turbulent character, he would be glad to be informed who was to become furety for my good behaviour while I remained in the country. I anfwered, that in ordinary cafes, the maxims of our police required no other pledge of a man's obedience to the laws, than his perfon and property. He replied, that a ferocity of mind, peculiar to Europeans, and wholly incompatible with the mild genius of the natives, had obliged him to difmifs fome of them from the country; but that to have recourfe to their perfons or property was a procefs which muft be attended with too much trouble and inconvenience. The fact was, that a few determined Europeans, in a late inftance, had put a large body of fepoys to flight, and, elated by their fuccefs, had proceeded to take poffeffion of feveral villages. Europeans are apt to entertain the falfe idea,
that

that they never can do enough in fupport of their national character for bravery, and hence are fometimes betrayed into the moft unwarrantable exceffes;—while, ftrange as it may feem, were thefe gallant Europeans, fo fuperior to the Moors of India, by fome unaccountable fatality to be placed in any province of the Ottoman empire, we fhould prefently find them the inferiors of the fame people, I mean the Moors of Turky.

This gentle difpofition of the natives of India is probably owing in a great degree to temperance, and a total abftinence from animal food. The common ufe of this diet, in the bulk of other nations in the world, has I believe exalted the natural tone of their paffions; and I can account upon no other principle for the ftrong harfh features of Muffulmen and Chriftians, compared with the fmall trait, and placid afpect of the Gentoo. Whoever has not had an opportunity of making this comparifon, may find it difficult to underftand what is meant by this relative coarfenefs of feature; but in the part of India where I now refide, it would be eafy to illuftrate it in

many

many inftances, by only placing together two natives of the fame province.

The manner of life led by a Bramin may, I have no doubt, contribute likewife to the fame effect. His refidence in the neighbourhood, but feldom within the walls, of a great town, is fixed in the midft of extenfive gardens; and this, by the bye, is the true reafon why the fea-coaft all the way from Trapore is bordered with garden-ground; and hence too the very populous ftate of that part of the country; whilft at Baffan, a large and well-fortified city, I met with military men only, whofe families were in the country. Now this retired and half folitary life of the Bramin deprives him of none of the innocent pleafures of fociety; but exempts him from a thoufand difagreeable and painful incidents, unavoidable to thofe who live within the walls of a city. The perpetual verdure of his retreat; the prefence of his trees and his flocks; an entire freedom from the irkfome ceremony infeparable from great focieties, whereby a man often finds himfelf hampered even in his own family; thefe, in
fhort,

short, and other circumstances, all tending to lead man back to his first and natural state, may account for that benign temper of mind, as well as for those peculiarities of feature, observable in the Bramin.

Their laws are the result of a truly meek and moral intellect, and I am told are excellently calculated to cherish and cultivate similar dispositions in the people. Professing myself, however, but little conversant in the Gentoo code, I shall mention only a very few of their political institutions :— Whoever refuses to pay a tax imposed by the authority of the public, is liable to be charged with a double rate, but is never on this account subjected to corporal punishment, that being reserved for the violations of man's natural rights: murder and assassination are punished with death; seduction in either sex with the forfeiture of liberty, and the loss of one eye; robbery with the amputation of one hand, and perpetual slavery;—these judicious laws render it very seldom necessary for the magistrate to exact penalties of a sanguinary nature. The principle of the political and moral

regu-

regulations of the Bramins is to allure man to his native innocence and fimplicity, to engage him to conform his actions to the firſt principles of his nature, and efpecially to abſtain from whatever may have a tndency to irritate or inflame his paſſions. This is the great object of the divine law; and ſhould the wiſdom of man try to accompliſh more, the experiment would unavoidably fail. I am likewife of opinion that the claſſing of men into different caſts, is an inſtitution calculated to produce the moſt pure and genuine manners.

Many of the obfervations which I made in the iſland of Samar I found not only applicable to this country, but even illuſtrated and confirmed by the lives of the Bramins, men whom, except in matters of religious opinion, I was in all refpects ambitious to imitate. Like the Bramin, my neighbour, my refidence was in the midſt of a large and beautiful garden, in which my hours glided fmoothly away in one quiet and uniform tenor. Rice, fruit, and vegetables, gathered and dreſſed with my own hands, a diet to which my ſtomach had been long accuſtomed, cuftomed, adminiftered to my daily fubfiftence. My travels had occafioned an extreme heat of blood, and this I was at pains to remove by drinking rice-broth, which, properly made, is equally palatable with the fineft milk. Two pieces of cotton cloth, the one a covering to my loins, and the other thrown over my fhoulders, compofed my ordinary drefs. I allowed my beard to grow in imitation of the higheft caft, and like them generally walked abroad with my head uncovered and my feet bare. In fituations requiring any ceremony I appeared in my full drefs, which confifted of a long white robe girt round the waift in the manner of the Marrattas, and a turban and fandals, in the Moorifh fafhion. My time was employed chiefly in reading, walking, and cultivating my garden. A few goats and fome poultry, which I found means to procure in the neighbourhood, contributed to my amufement; and I occafionally made vifits in the adjacent villages. Agreeably to the manners of the country, I paffed the night on a mat of reeds, the

cool

cool and temperate effect of which afforded me the moſt ſalutary and refreſhing repoſe.

This courſe of life, which I purſued with much ſatisfaction for a conſiderable time, was ſo analogous to the manners of the Gentoo, and ſo different from thoſe of an European, that it ſoon procured me the credit and reputation of a ſincere penitent. The Bramin, as well as the Chriſtian, began to regard me with an eye of veneration. I was viſited, invited to all entertainments, and every body ſeemed ambitious of my acquaintance. I received preſents of the choiceſt fruits from the neighbouring gardens; and, in ſhort, came to be eſteemed a moſt devout man, who was employed in expiating his ſins by the rigorous auſterities of a new life. But, alas! my virtues were far from meriting the high encomiums they received; and I was in the painful and humiliating ſituation of a man who muſt hear himſelf praiſed for certain good or great qualities, which he is inwardly conſcious he does not poſſeſs.

I had

I had the misfortune to be seized with a diforder named fernas, pretty common in this country, which is accompanied with large puftules on the body and hands. Thofe on the fingers occafioned the lofs of four of my nails. At the end of twenty days, after having tried various remedies in ufe among the natives, finding myfelf ftill greatly indifpofed, I fet out for Surat, hoping to receive more benefit from the medical fkill of the capital. The fatigue of the journey, change of air, and, above all, the advantage of fea-bathing, difcharged my pimples; and I began to find myfelf confiderably better.

CHAP. VI.

Probity and hospitality of the Gentoos.—Their carnival described.—The Author arrives at Surat.—Its situation, extensive commerce, and flourishing state of the inhabitants.—Splendid stile of living of a private merchant.—Magnificent display of the Nabob on a public occasion.

FIVE months had now elapsed since I came to reside in the country, during which period I went frequently abroad, and made excursions in all directions, without encountering the smallest danger. The civil reception I every where experienced from the inhabitants, I am inclined to impute partly to my complexion, which fatigue and the influence of hot climates had rendered similar to their own, and partly to my dress, which was entirely accommodated to the taste of the natives. The only language in which I could make myself understood was the Portuguese, which, though

though somewhat in ufe in the country, is far from being generally fpoken; hence, on various occafions, I was taken for a Hindoo. In all fituations, however, I was equally the object of confidence and hofpitality. It is evident that the crimes of theft and robbery muft be extremely rare, fince, in the courfe of fo many months, a fingle inftance of either did not come to my knowledge; and though I was on different occafions three or four days from home, when, according to the cuftom of the country, the door of my cottage was left open, I never had the flighteft reafon to fuppofe that a ftranger had croffed the threfhold in my abfence.

In thofe countries, I have obferved, where the people are nearly upon a footing in point of property, the private rights of individuals are leaft liable to be invaded; for, by this means, a certain defcription of evil propenfities, which grow out of arbitrary diftinctions, and increafe in violence with the unequal diftribution of property, are evidently precluded.

I was

I was at Pardy on the day of the Gentoos' carnival. On this occafion thefe people run about the ftreets, with their faces and cloaths begrimed with powders of different colours. Dancing to harfh inftruments, and imparting to all who came in their way the fame ridiculous appearance with their own, feemed to be the chief objects of their amufement. Next day I lodged at Naufary, in the gardens of a rich Perfian, who, in the true fpirit of hofpitality, had erected a magnificent tent in the midft of a beautiful parterre, for the reception and entertainment of ftrangers. On the enfuing day, being the 19th of March, I arrived at Surat, and alighted at the French factory. I embraced the conful's obliging offer of accommodation in his family; and waited a whole month for the failing of a Moorifh veffel, which an eminent merchant of Surat was equipping for the trade of Baffora. By this means I had an opportunity of obtaining a more perfect knowledge of this harbour, by far the moft confiderable in the poffeffion of the natives. The commerce of European nations

tions in India was formerly confined to a few factories at this port; and I am of opinion, it would have been fortunate for both parties, had there exifted, in convenient fituations on the Indian coaft, other fuch confiderable cities as Surat. The power of the Indian princes, in thefe circumftances, would have operated with more effect, and might have checked that fpirit of conqueft in Europeans, which, partly owing to the calamities infeparable from war, but chiefly to the fad diminution it occafions in the induftry of the people, muft always prove difaftrous to the proper views of a trading company. The commerce of Canton has been uniformly carried on nearly upon equal terms with all nations whatever; and the Chinefe trade continues ftill to maintain its ground in a manner advantageous both to the native and foreigner, a fact which I confider as an illuftration and proof of the truth of my opinion.

Surat ftands in a large and fertile plain, with few trees, particularly on the left fide of the river, and commands a view of the oppofite grounds. The ftreets are of confiderable breadth; but aukwardly formed, miferably paved, and, from the various induftry of a crouded population, extremely inconvenient. The houfes are large and ftrongly built, in good tafte, and well fuited to the climate; though with very little outwardly to recommend them. The public markets of every denomination are well fupplied with all the neceffaries and comforts of life. The incredible number of flaves and fepoys, it being permitted to every individual to have as many armed men in his fervice as he can afford to pay, and the concourfe of coaches and palanquins, imprefs the mind of a ftranger with a high idea of the affluence of the people. The cabriole, but in the Moorifh tafte, is as common at Surat as is that vehicle in the ftreets of London or Paris; and, as it is drawn by oxen trained to go at a gallop, is equally convenient and expeditious: the pole and harnefs of the carriage are made of bamboo, and have all the elafticity of our main-braces. The gardens are many and beautiful. The harbour is greatly frequented;

quented; and the ſhips built in their dockyards are of a ſtrong and ſolid conſtruction. The trade of Surat, ſtill very extenſive, has, however, been much impaired by certain impolitic regulations introduced by the nabob, at the inſtigation of the Engliſh.

This being the great mart for the immenſe produce of one of the richeſt and moſt extenſive parts of India, the quantity and variety of merchandize diſplayed in the warehouſes are aſtoniſhing to a ſtranger. Beſides the European factories, there are here Mooriſh, Perſian, and Gentoo merchants; and, in order that the reader may have an idea of a merchant of Surat, I ſhall juſt mention the proprietor of the ſhip on board which I had taken a paſſage for Baſſora. His trade, it is proper to obſerve, had decreaſed to leſs than one half of what it had been formerly; but he was ſtill owner of ten large armed veſſels, which he let out on freight to the Engliſh. From his ſlaves he obtained agents and ſupercargoes for his factories abroad, and ſometimes captains and officers for the veſſels he equipped and employed on

his

his own account. His ſhips, as well as his factory at Baſſora, diſplayed his flag; and he poſſeſſed, as a ſovereignty, a conſiderable iſland in the Euphrates. His commercial operations extended over the whole Indian coaſt, from China to Baſſora. In his family were at leaſt a hundred ſlaves of ſome diſtinction, who had ſlaves under them. I ſaw him on a day of unuſual ceremony, when he appeared mounted on an elephant, and, beſides a long train of dependants on foot, was attended by a numerous company of his own relations on horſeback, and in palanquins. Two hundred of his ſepoys led the van, while a large collection of muſical inſtruments, braying intolerable diſſonance, cloſed the rear; a proceſſion which, in my opinion, would have better ſuited the emperor of Java than a dealer in callicoes at Surat.

I attended the commemoration of Abraham's ſacrifice, or the Courbanbeyran, a ſolemnity to which the extraordinary pomp of the Indian grandees in their attendance on the nabob to his moſque, the incredible number of troops, the bands of muſic, the

ſplen-

splendour of equipages and robes, and the immense croud of spectators assembled from all quarters, gave peculiar grandeur and magnificence. His highness was escorted by five or six thousand sepoys, and a considerable train of artillery, whilst between him and his mufti, the English counsellors, with a body of the company's troops, took distinguished precedence.

It is sometimes difficult to say in which of these powers, the English, the Marrattas, or the nabob, the supreme authority is vested; and hence, in the course of my travels, I have never met with an equal number of armed men in any other city in the world. The English are in possession of the castle and certain gates, the nabob is nominally master of the city, and the Marrattas, who claim a kind of tribute annually from the inhabitants, have two gates and a large body of troops; but, from this aukward collision of divided authority, there frequently arises much public violence and disorder. I shall here conclude my observations on Surat, the grandeur of which, though in a stile extremely

dif-

different from all that I have ever feen in Europe, has fomething about it, however, peculiarly ſtriking, and impoſing on the imagination.

CHAP. VII.

The Author leaves Surat, and arrives by ſea at Maſcate in Arabia Felix.—Sound policy of the Iman or ſovereign of this kingdom.—Departure from Maſcate for the Perſian Gulf.—Singular cuſtom of the Indian mariners in the Straits of Ormus.

ON the 20th of April we ſailed for Baſſora, in company with an Engliſh armed veſſel, which ſerved us for a pilot and convoy to the mouth of the gulf. She was deſtined to free the coaſts from the *Sindys* and *Chamchas*, not from Marratta pirates, as is commonly ſuppoſed. The good government of the Marratta tribes, and particularly their unremitting induſtry to repreſs piracy in thoſe ſeas, by their forts

forts and cruizers, to which even the Portuguefe flag owes its protection, renders it extremely improbable that the freebooters who moleft the Malabar coaft, and who are generally called Marratta pirates, actually belong to thofe ftates. It is poffible, indeed, that they may defcend from the fouthern parts of the Marratta dominions; but in this cafe, unowned and unencouraged by that government, they fkulk under the flag of the little difaffected princes, who are very frequent on thofe coafts.

Being to touch at Mafcate, and as the S. W. winds were faft approaching, and the direction of the current bore towards the coaft of Sindys or Diu, we fteered weftward, and made the land of a low and fandy fhore, S.W. of the Refulgat mountains. We then coafted northward, and dropped anchor at Mafcate, after a paffage of thirteen days. Befides a large and excellent road, there is here a very good harbour, in which we found four fathoms and a half of water. The high mountains of the coaft and adjacent iflands, by which the harbour is formed, cover it from the winds,

and

and protect it in all seasons from the inconvenience of a rolling sea. S. W. from the heights of cape Refulgat, and on that part of the coast where we landed, is another port; but it is only frequented by the Arabs, the Abyssinians, and the trade of the Red Sea. Mascate is without the streights of Ormus, and consequently in a most favourable situation for trade. Hence it serves as an emporium for the commerce of Indus, whose straits are frequently rough and tempestuous, as well as for that of the Persian gulf, whose navigation is much more tedious and uncertain than that of the Indian sea.

Our pilot, though an Indian Moor, was a man of good capacity; he settled with great facility the ship's course, but by rules different from ours, which I cannot pretend to explain: he gave his orders with much compofure and precifion; and navigated the vessel by charts, which he himself had drawn of the Chinese gulf of Bengal and Persia. Had the natural talents of this Moor been cultivated by the science of mathematics, and had he possessed in a
higher

higher degree the enterprize of a European navigator, I am fatisfied he would have made an excellent feaman.

I took the earlieft opportunity of going afhore, and met with a native of Hifpahan, who acted as agent for French affairs in this city. The Arabian populace have generally been reprefented as a wicked and licentious race of men; a report which, as I went about in town and country, in an European drefs, without meeting with the fmalleft difturbance, my own experience by no means warrants me to confirm. In this town, which, by the bye, is miferably built, I faw a number of fine gardens. Befides trefoil, and as many vegetables as a fcanty foil, lying among barren rocks, may be expected to produce, there are here dates, apricots, and fig-trees, both of India and Europe. The roots and vegetables are equal to the confumption of ftrangers as well as the inhabitants. This port is frequented by fhipping from the different countries of India; but particularly by thofe employed in the coafting trade from Eleatif all the way to Ceylon.

The quiet manners of the Arabians in this city, proceed probably from their intercourse with strangers, and from their being accustomed to mingle with people of all religions, as well as from the good policy of the Iman or sovereign, who is anxious to promote the interests of trade and navigation in every part of his dominions. Besides, it is still recollected that this country once belonged to the Portuguese, and that coercive means have occasionally been employed to controul the restless humour of the natives; and hence the reason, I presume, why Europeans experience a degree of consideration here, which they do not enjoy in any other part of Arabia. The Iman is too sensible of the advantages of their commerce, to discourage them from entering his harbour; but he is also jealous of their conduct, and too careful of his own security to permit them to settle in his town. He knows, that although Mascate is situated on the mainland of Arabia, it is, however, in a manner separated from the continent by very high and inaccessible mountains, and he therefore trembles at the thought

thought of admitting an European colony within the walls of a city, which has no communication with his other dominions, except by a narrow pafs among fteep and rugged rocks; where a handful of men might eafily ftop the progrefs of a whole army.

The Iman of this kingdom affects to be the only real defcendant of Mahomet, and therefore wears a blue, inftead of the green turban which is worn by the cheiks of Turkey. He is fovereign of an extenfive country, and refides in his capital, fituated behind lofty and barren mountains, at five days journey from Mafcate. Paffing the mountains of Mafcate, the traveller defcends into a vaft plain covered with date trees, interfperfed with herds of cattle and fruitful fields, and cultivated by a people of civil and obliging manners. Such is the information, at leaft, which I received from a French factor, who, in order to avoid the heat of Mafcate, which the reflection of the mountains, and the fcarcity of rain in the dry feafon, render almoft uninhabitable, paffes the fummer months in that country.

Vol. II.   F   Rain

Rain never falls oftener in this part of the world than four or perhaps five times in the year.

In thefe regions the bulk of the inhabitants live chiefly on dates and milk, converted into a very dry fubftance, with the appearance of little flint ftones; which, however, being again diffolved, afford a kind of acid, but refrefhing liquor. The environs of Mafcate, which are confined by their contiguity to thefe high naked mountains, produce nothing but a few vegetables. From the fea, however, they are well fupplied with fifh, while all other articles of fubfiftence are imported either by fea from Sindys and Perfia, or upon the backs of mules from the interior parts of the country.

I obferved both at Batavia and Surat, that the Afiatic women, efpecially the Mahometans, appear very feldom abroad. At Surat, the body as well as the face of the women is covered by a veil; but at Mafcate thefe oriental manners are obferved with fuch extreme rigour, that not even in a fhop or public market is an Arabian female

to

to be feen. During my abode in this city I did not obferve an individual of the moft amiable part of our fpecies, three negroe flaves excepted, and they were wrapped up in large linen cloaks.

Having fpent feveral days at this port, one of the moft commercial in Arabia Felix, we got a pilot for the Perfian Gulf, and weighing anchor ftood for the Straits of Ormus, which we came in view of in the fpace of forty-eight hours; but as the wind blew from the N. W. frefh and fqually, in order to clear the ifles of Ormus and Mamouth Salem, we were obliged to keep tacking for feveral days.

The terror of a tremendous rolling fea, which prevails in the Straits of Ormus, has given rife to a very fingular cuftom practifed by the Indian mariners. On a certain day of the year they conftruct, as a prefent for and in order to appeafe the wrath of Mamouth Salem, a fmall veffel, which, upon entering the Straits, they launch into the waves, fatisfied that by this fymbolical fhipwreck they elude the fury of that vengeance which was pointed

againft

againſt themſelves. To this rite of ſuperſtition ſucceeds a mock naval engagement, in which the brave exertions of the natives to defend the entrance to their ſeas againſt the invaſions of the enemy, are meant to be repreſented; when the former, after diſplaying many feats of heroic valour, are conſtantly victorious.

We ſoon diſcovered a cape on the coaſt of Perſia, which forms a kind of elbow, and determines the entrance to the Straits. I had been told it was uſual to ſail immediately round it; but our pilot was of a different opinion, and choſe to ſtand towards the other ſide, keeping at ſeveral leagues diſtance from the coaſt of Arabia. I cannot, however, give him much credit for his ability as a ſeaman on this occaſion, for next day the wind ſhifted to the N. W. and blew freſh with violent ſqualls. It was now the ſeaſon when the N. W. winds prevail in the Perſian Gulf, and as they continue to blow during the ſummer months, the paſſage of the Straits was become extremely precarious. We entered the Sound, which continues all the way to

Baſſora;

Baſſora; and having diſcovered the coaſt of Bender Abaſſy, a port much frequented in former times, we ſtood along the ſide of a little iſland ſituated S. W. of *Camron* or *Kiſmiſs*, between which two places lies a paſſage into the Straits. The wind favouring us a little, we coaſted the iſland of *Camron* on the ſide next the ſea. As we advanced, the courſe of the current, which iſſues from the mouth of the gulf, as well as the N. W. wind, which blew conſtantly till we reached Baſſora, were againſt us. We ſailed, therefore, at the diſtance of only five or ſix leagues from the coaſt of Perſia, in order to keep as much as poſſible in the line of ſeparation between the N. W. wind, which blows towards the coaſt of Arabia, and is eſteemed extremely unwholeſome, and that ſtormy region which lies along the Perſian ſhore. We had at times favourable intervals, and continuing the ſame courſe we left three iſlands towards the coaſt of Arabia, but kept conſtantly at the ſame diſtance from the ſide of Perſia, being apprehenſive of meeting with ſtorms or calms under the adjacent mountains.

CHAP. VIII.

Character of the Dervifes and Moorifh Muſſulmen of Afia.—The opinion the Afiatics in general entertain of Europeans.—Singular mathematical demonſtration of the Indian philoſophers.—The Author arrives at Bender Abouchier, in Perfia.

I LIVED on the beſt terms with our Moorifh paſſengers, whoſe meek and peaceable difpofition harmonized with my own. They appeared fomewhat fanatical in matters of religion, as indeed are all Muſſulmen of great towns, but I was careful to give them no offence in their exerciſes, for while they ſaid prayers and read the *Koran* at my fide, I made it my bufinefs never to be found between their proftrations and the prophet's grave at Mecca. Their complaifant behaviour was not confined to Muſſulmen, but extended equally to Gentoos, Chriſtians, and Jews, a liberality which ſoftened in ſome degree the harſh opinion I had been uſed to entertain

tertain of all who had imbibed the haughty and imperious doctrines of Mahomet. The first principles of that law, though severe and intolerant as to manners, are in many respects just; but the system being upon the whole a transcript of the prejudices and narrow character of its founder, tends to inculcate in the minds of its votaries a superlative notion of superiority over other men. The friendly and sociable behaviour, therefore, of these Moors, I would refer partly to the native character of the Asiatic, and partly to the least exceptionable maxims and institutions of their religion.

We had likewise twenty Dervises, whose deportment was in every respect congenial to their profession, and engaged my sincere veneration. From their conversation I could discover in these men the soundest principles of morality, which their painful situation during this voyage gave them frequent occasion to exercise. One of their companions, who lay ill, after suffering extreme agony, which he bore with great constancy and resignation, shewed, in a mild and serene countenance, at the moment of his diffolution, with how little regret he bade adieu to this frail and miferable life. For the edification of the company during our repafts, the beft informed among the Dervifes were regularly invited by the fhip's officers to read and explain different paffages of their books; but thefe lectures I ufed to find of a very tirefome length. On fuch occafions I enjoyed the agreeable fociety of a Jew, a native of Aden, who was not inferior to any of our paffengers in the meek and moral virtues of the Afiatic; and with whom I had much fatisfaction in difcuffing the grounds of our different religious opinions.

The fhip's officers feemed to be of an inquifitive difpofition, and hence, among many other queftions, I was afked, why the French in general were fo little addicted to the fame fimple way of thinking and acting as myfelf; whence arofe that extreme impatience, which hurried them to the ends of the earth, amaffing money, and fpending it to no manner of purpofe; and what pleafure or amufement they could find in being the inftruments of animosity

and

and diffenfion in all the nations which had the misfortune to receive their vifits? They expreffed much regret that the Europeans had been fo fuccefsful in feducing the natives of Afia to their interefts and views, the pernicious effects of which they alledged were now felt, when it was too late to remedy them. I talked a great deal of the glory of the *Grande Monarque*, and the dignity as well as fecurity of the ftate: but they could entertain no notion of glory, or even of duty, when feparated from moral rectitude, and the principles of a fimple and charitable mind. I will not pretend to fay which opinion prevailed in point of argument; but it was evident, that though they feemed extremely candid and open to information, I had not the honour to bring them over to my fide of the queftion.

The Afiatics in general confider Europeans as men of reafoning, rather than reafonable men; or, in other words, as a race of ingenious fools; and in this opinion our whole fhip's company feemed to concur. According to them, in order to
form

form a right judgment of any thing, a man should assume the character of a judge, divested of all bias and interest whatever with regard to the point in discussion. He must possess the faculty of a just and luminous understanding, with what they term an unimpaired elasticity of brain; requisites seldom to be found in a man of business, the bent of whose mind is too much directed towards one object, and never, they contend, to be found in an European, whose prejudiced habits of life are wholly incompatible with freedom of reflection and sound judgment. The reasoning of these people did not appear to me to be altogether false; but when I considered their indolence, and our weakness, the difference between us appeared to be only in degree; for it is impossible that human candour and impartiality should ever reach so high a standard, as that all the sentiments of even the best men shall be true, and exactly conformable to the nature of things.

Although these men were by no means adepts in the science of geometry, they affected to ascertain the feat of just thought
by

by a very fingular kind of mathematical illuftration. This, they fay, is to be found
on the vertex of a very obtufe angle, formed
by two lines, the extremities of which at
the point of contact reprefent fenfe and
reafon. The other extremities of the
lines, on account of the fpecies of angle
they contain, are almoft oppofite to each
other, and denote folly in oppofition to
fenfe, and ftupidity in oppofition to reafon;
—now the moment a man recedes from the
angular point where fenfe and reafon are
united, and where nature originally placed
him, he begins to approximate to the extreme, either of folly or ftupidity. In their
application of this problem, the natives of
both countries deal uncandidly with each
other; for while the Afiatic finds the European at the pinnacle of folly, the European is equally fure he difcovers the Afiatic
in the extreme point of ftupidity. For
my part, I am perfuaded that neither the
one nor the other is in a condition to maintain his balance on the angular point. And
therefore to man, liable as he is to be furprized and agitated by all the violent paffions

fions of his nature, the ftation affigned him by the Indian philofopher muft ever afford a precarious fupport. But I return to the fequel of my voyage.

We touched at Bender Abouchier, a fea port of Perfia, where, after executing the inftructions of our employers, we were to receive a new pilot. The firft pilot belonged to Mafcate, and had engaged to conduct us for fifty rupees to Abouchier only. We were now to enter the channel of the Euphrates, the navigation of which this pilot did not pretend to underftand, and it was plain he was but a novice in the practical part of his profeffion; for at the diftance of twenty leagues from Abouchier the fhip got entangled among rocks, which project from a certain cape far into the fea, and by this accident we were confiderably detained. While we were ftruggling with our difficulties amidft thefe rocks, at leaft five leagues from land, the wind, which never veered from the N. W. fprung up frefh and fqually, and we were obliged to drop an anchor in twenty fathoms water, two leagues from the fhore. A calm

calm now enfued, and we again got under weigh, and at length doubled the cape, after which the coaſt begins to recede towards the N. E.; but we ſpent twelve days in recovering the advantage we had loſt by the ignorance of our pilot. We now ſtood with the rocks of the cape on our right, and a ſmall iſland with ſeveral adjacent ſand-banks on the larboard ſide. Theſe rocks are very incorrectly laid down on our charts, which indeed are in general extremely inaccurate reſpecting the navigation of this gulf. Six days after, as we paſſed a fort, formerly in poſſeſſion of the Portugueſe, we entered the road of Abouchier, which is much expoſed, but has an excellent bottom.

In the mouth of the port lay a veſſel belonging to Great Britain, the only European nation which trades here. The entrance to the harbour being formed by banks of ſand, extending a great way into the gulf, is difficult of acceſs: the road is, beſides, at too great a diſtance from the land, and the coaſt is exceſſively low towards the edge of the ſea.

From

From this plentiful country, which is regarded as the granary of Baffora, we received an excellent fupply of provifions. The foil immediately about Baffora, as well as the adjacent country, being miferably dry and barren, its inhabitants are indebted for the neceffaries of life to Bender Abouchier, whofe environs are remarkably fertile and pleafant.

CHAP. IX.

Anchorage on the coaft of the ifland of Careith.—Paffage from thence to the mouth of the Euphrates.—Defcription of this river and the Curd Coaft.—Arrival at Baffora.

HAVING taken on board a pilot for the further profecution of our voyage, in confideration of whofe trouble and the ufe of a founding boat we were to pay thirty rupees, we again put to fea with a favourable wind, and ftood for the mouth

of

of the Euphrates. We had proceeded little more than three leagues and a half, for we had not yet doubled the ifland of Careith, when the wind returning to the N. W. blew frefh, and exceffively hot. We tacked, but without gaining the fmalleft advantage; and the wind continuing to blow with the fame force, feconded by the current, and our water, of which we had laid in none at Abouchier, beginning to fail, we came to anchor at Careith. The fovereignty of this ifland belongs to a Perfian chief, who pays tribute to the prince of Bender Abouchier. This prince likewife receives tribute from the little ifland of Barheim, famous for its pearl-fifheries. The empire of Perfia, like that of the Mogul, is broken into fmall principalities, which are held and acknowledged by their refpective lords as fiefs under the prince of Hifpahan.

The ifle of Careith, which once belonged to the Dutch, and which the Englifh in a later period endeavoured to become mafters of, is at prefent inhabited by Perfians, Curds, and Arabs, who all agree in one point, viz.

a moft

a moſt rooted antipathy to Europeans. The Careith veſſels, which infeſt the Perſian Gulf, are like our gallies; and though they are ſcarcely conſidered in the light of pirates, every European trader ought to be well armed and in condition to face them. Preſuming, at firſt ſight, that we belonged to ſome European port, they gave chace, and ſtopped our ſhip's boat; but, upon diſcovering that our's was an Indian veſſel, the boat was releaſed, and we were permitted to proſecute our voyage.

The inhabitants of Abouchier itſelf are far from being in the intereſt of Europeans, and hence the bottom of the gulf from Barheim to Abouchier is frequented by a number of ſmall veſſels, a ſort of ſemi-pirates, againſt which ſuch ſhips from Europe as have buſineſs in theſe ſeas would do well to be on their guard. Though we had been provided with a pilot for the Euphrates at Abouchier, we were obliged to hire another at Careith; and as a part of his ſalary is a perquiſite to government, it was idle to inſiſt upon the inutility of two pilots for the ſame voyage. Having therefore,

fore, according to Afiatic cuftom, made him a prefent over and above his wages, and received another in return, we again fet fail. As the coaft lies extremely low, and is bordered all along with flooded grounds, it was with great difficulty, and by conftantly heaving the lead, our pilots being very unfkilful, that we at laft reached the mouth of the river. At the diftance of eight leagues from the Euphrates, the pilots, I obferved, became anxious about what they called the entrance to the old bed of the river, which is fituated on the Curd coaft. We paffed over various banks and gutters, along which the river difcharges itfelf into the gulf, and were twice a-ground, notwithftanding the attention of our pilots, before we could reach the coaft of Arabia. We fent the boat and fome of our hands on fhore, in queft of the date-tree; for as it is not produced on the confines of the other paffages, it is by this means they are enabled to afcertain the principal channel of the river. We foon found a date branch, which encouraged our pilots, and they entered boldly into the channel.

As this paſſage runs in a line parallel to the ſhore, as ſoon as the veſſel gets ſight of the land, which, however, is extremely low, ſhe is known to be clear of all thoſe banks that incommode the navigation of the Euphrates. Beſides the inconvenience of a very rapid current, there are but twenty feet water at flood tide in the deepeſt of thoſe channels, which run between the ſand-banks formed in the bed of the river. It is neceſſary in theſe narrow channels to be particularly careful not to run a-ground; for, being expoſed in this ſituation to the whole force of the current, the veſſel would be in danger of going to pieces. When the pilot is apprehenſive, therefore, of ſuch an accident, he endeavours to lay the ſhip in a cavity of the bank, where, as the force of the current has been already broken in its deſcent, ſhe may remain in tolerable ſafety.

The Curd coaſt being formed entirely of ſunken grounds, I am inclined to believe that the other paſſages up the Euphrates, mentioned by ſome navigators, are extremely narrow; at leaſt, I can ſay that in ſailing up up this river I did not find, and I have not heard that there is any other very considerable channel.

The dry and sandy coast of Arabia is a certain mark of the branch we pursued; but we had steered along this coast a considerable time, when we arrived at the extremity of the river's opposite bank, which is on the Curd side greenish, and ought to be in view before the pilot attempts to enter into the middle of the channel. The vessel no sooner gets between the banks of the Euphrates, than the depth of water is found to be considerably increased. As Bassora is at the distance of forty leagues from the sea, ships sail up with the tide, and anchor at Jusan in any place they please, unmolested by the current. At Jusan the bottom is good, and of a greenish clay, but of so tenacious a quality, that it is often difficult to weigh anchor: for about twenty-five leagues from the mouth of the river, it is tolerably neat and clean, but it begins there to be incommoded by sand-banks, which render the navigation very difficult.

The Euphrates detaches, on the fide of Arabia, a fmall channel navigable for craft of fifty tons, along which are villages that trade with Baffora, and Elcatif, a town of Arabia, fituated in the line of the channel. We continued our courfe along the coaft of Arabia; but found it neceffary to proceed with the greateft circumfpection, particularly where the fhore is low, as it is fometimes without date-trees, and overflowed at high water.

We paffed a mofque of Dervifes on the Curd coaft, and afterwards the ruins of fome old fortifications, acrofs which and the oppofite bank Solimancha, a famous Curd chieftain, threw chains and a bridge of boats, when he intercepted the navigation of the Euphrates. About fix leagues from Baffora, we paffed to the left of the little ifland of Cheliby, and afterwards difcovered, on the coaft of Arabia, the mouth of a fmall river, on the banks of which ftands an inconfiderable mofque. Here, at a third of the river's breadth from the Arabian coaft, the Baffora fhipping come to anchor.

anchor. On the border of this river, and only a quarter of a league within the extremities of its banks, ſtands the city of Baſſora, whoſe gardens extend to the very edge of the Euphrates.

CHAP. X.

Deſcription of the city of Baſſora.—Politic conduct of the Engliſh in obtaining a footing there.—The Author quits Baſſora to join a caravan of Arabian ſhepherds for Aleppo.

AT this place we found three armed ſhips belonging to Great Britain, which were deſtined for the protection of the Engliſh at Baſſora, Aboucheir, and Maſcate, as well as to defend their trade from the depredations of the natives in the navigation of the gulf. The Engliſh poſſeſs the greateſt part of the Baſſora trade; but as the Arabs and Curds, who compoſe the

bulk

bulk of the inhabitants, are little civilized, and as the Turks, from their remote fituation from Europe, might be tempted to expel ftrangers, with a view to a monopoly of this trade, the Englifh have had the addrefs, under various pretexts, to get five hundred national troops ftationed on fhore. Befides, as their fhips lie at anchor within lefs than a gun-fhot of the town, they are in condition to over-awe the inhabitants upon any emergency that may render their interference expedient. The Arabian populace are generally confidered, as has been already obferved, fpiteful and vindictive to ftrangers, particularly Europeans; I have feen, however, Indian failors in the fervice of the Englifh give law to the natives of Baffora, by a fevere application of the oar. This behaviour would have been very differently received from the hirelings of any other nation; but it is a common obfervation, that the arrogance of a powerful mafter often defcends to his fervant; hence, though naturally tame and unwarlike in his own character, he will affect a fuperiority over thofe who, on ordinary occafions, are much braver

than

than himself. In the exercife of a moft
extenfive commerce, the Englifh have difcovered the good policy of appearing open
and liberal in their tranfactions with ftrangers; and therefore, though their conduct, in other refpects, often gives umbrage,
they are efteemed as merchants.

Baffora is a large and populous city; but
the town-walls, as well as the private houfes,
which are fmall and mean, are built entirely of earth. The houfes are either altogether without windows, or have them
of a very diminutive fize, in order to ex-
clude the burning winds of the defert, which
arife from under the walls of the town.
The banks of the Euphrates fupply the
inhabitants with fruit and vegetables, while
they receive from Perfia and Bender Aboucheir all the other neceffaries of life. The
bulk of the people, like the reft of the
natives in this quarter of Arabia, fubfift almoft entirely on dates and a kind of four
milk. The cuftoms of the Eaft, refpecting
the females, are obferved here in all their
ftrictnefs; infomuch that, from the condition of children to that of full-grown women,

men, they are equally invifible to the eye of a ftranger as if they were entirely extinct.

Baffora is fubject, under the Grand Signior, to the Bafha of Bagdad, who, however, poffeffes but a very limited authority, and finds it expedient to exercife much difcretion in his conduct towards both the Curds and Arabians. There are here feveral Jewifh and Arabian merchants, who trade with Aboucheir, Mafcate, Barheim, and Elcatif, and efpecially with the ifle of Barheim, which fupplies the Elcatif merchants, as well as thofe of the towns on the canal above mentioned, with beautiful pearls.

In the regions of the defert immediately contiguous to this city are Cheiks or Arabian Chieftains, who entertain a violent averfion to the Mahometans, and who worfhip one God, without regard to myftery, or any fyftematic form of worfhip whatever. The other inhabitants in thefe parts, particularly on the confines of the defert, are rigid followers of the prophet; but I am told, that in more interior fituations

there

there are feveral ignorant tribes, half Jews and half Chriftians, who adhere to no defined clafs of religious opinions in the world.

Having quitted the fhip before fhe arrived at her ftation, I got on fhore the 25th of June, 1770, and was well received by the French conful, who politely made me a tender of his fervices. Learning that fifteen days before a very rich and numerous caravan had fet out for Aleppo, I faw with much regret that our tedious paflage from Surat had deprived me of an excellent opportunity of crofling the defert; and was extremely apprehenfive that I might be obliged to wait fix months at Baffora for the departure of another. The merchants of this place carry on a confiderable traffic, by means of large boats decked with leather, deep in the hull, and built of the date-tree, (which is the only thing like timber in this country) with all that part of Afia, under the dominion of the Porte, which communicates with the Tygris and Euphrates.

The

The induftry of the people is obfervable in a fpecies of curious little boats, which they equip for the navigation of the river. They are of an oval form, made of ofiers interwoven in the manner of a bafket, and coated with mud and tar. They are very properly named *couffes*, and move by means of a kind of oar or fcull, prefenting a mode of navigation which I had fcarcely met with before.

My fears of being long detained at this ftage of my travels were of fhort continuance; for, agreeably to information I had received at Surat, I was told the day after my arrival, that a caravan of Bedouins, or Arabian fhepherds, on their way to Aleppo with young camels, were encamped two days journey from Baffora. Upon the caravan's halting in the neighbourhood, their chief had fent to make enquiry in the city whether there were any paffengers who defired to take the advantage of his protection over the defert. Some Arabians in the vicinity embraced this opportunity of going to Aleppo, from one of whom

this

the French conful was fo obliging as to hire me a dromedary, and to agree with him for the carriage of my water and effects, at the fame time ftipulating with another for his fervices as a cook. The Moorifh veffel not being come into port, I made all poffible hafte to fetch my things from on board, and to lay in fuch provifions as were neceffary for the journey. I dreffed myfelf in a Turkifh habit, and, having made my beft acknowledgments to my friend the conful for all his civilities, I took my leave and departed.

CHAP.

CHAP. XI.

The Author sets out with the Caravan on his journey through the Desert.—An Arabian encampment is discovered.—Curious ceremonies at meeting, betwixt the Arabs and the Bedouin shepherds.—The Author visits the Arabian camp, and describes the pursuits and mode of life of the Arabs.

MY stay at Bassora was only three days, and I joined the caravan on the 28th of June. In the evening we put up at a built* village, where I met with the Arabian with whom the consul had made the agreement, and from whom I received a written obligation for my safe conduct to Aleppo. He took me under his care with every mark of hospitality, and my entertainment began to favour rather more of the shepherd than town life. Next day the brother of my Arabian friend having ac-

* In contradistinction to the moveable habitations of the desert.

quainted

quainted me that every thing was ready for our departure, I mounted a camel, for the first time in my life, in company with eight Arabs. We began our march, and came up in the evening with our caravan, near a Bedouin camp, consisting of Arabs who sojourn in these parts. Our caravan amounted to a hundred and fifty men, and fifteen hundred young camels. The desert seemed entirely covered with herds and flocks of various denominations, belonging to the Bedouins of the neighbouring camp. The camels wander over the desert during the day in search of food, but are accustomed to join the camp in the evening, each repairing to his master's tent, before which he squats down until morning. From their milk and fleeces the Arab derives all the simple necessaries of life, food, cloathing, and lodging.

The day following we set forward on our journey, when the great extent of ground covered by the caravan afforded a very beautiful and entertaining prospect. On the second day of our march we passed the ruins of an old castle in the vicinity of a well,

well, out of which we filled our bottles; and in two days more we came to other wells, and overtook a couple of Arabs mounted on asses.

On the eighth day of our journey, we discovered an Arabian encampment; and here, in order to prevent my being distinguished from my companions, I put on an *abe* or robe, with a handkerchief floating on my head, in the style of the Arabs of the desert; for hitherto I had been clad in the Turkish fashion, which is different from that of the Arabs, particularly the Bedouins. The *abe* is made of woollen stuff, and composes the dress of both sexes. Next the skin is generally worn a white one of a fine quality, over which are two others of a larger size; and while the uppermost remains loose and flowing, the second is fastened about the waist with a girdle. The latter is commonly striped black and white; but the former is for the greatest part entirely black. This robe is of a very simple form, and, in order that the reader may have a distinct idea of it, he has only to conceive a sack of an equal width and length, which,

being

being flit lengthways for the convenience of putting it on, and paffed over the head, with two holes, one in each corner, to receive the arms, will be an exact model of the Arabian *abe*. This is all the variety of drefs that enters into the wardrobe of the Arab; his perfon, however, is completely covered, and his *abe* being of fo clofe a texture as to be impenetrable to water, is an excellent defence againft rain; and, as it is large enough to give free circulation to the air, and denfe enough to repel the firft blufh of the fun's rays, it is equally ufeful againft the burning heat of the defert. No perfon wears either breeches or drawers, as is cuftomary in towns. On the head of the male is an ample fized handkerchief of filk and cotton, attached to a large piece of cotton cloth, which, after paffing twice round the head, falls upon the fhoulders, covering them by its breadth. The ends of the handkerchief having been doubled down on the mouth and nofe, are returned under the fillet which binds it to the head, and in this manner the Arab endeavours to defend his cheft and lungs

lungs againſt the dangerous influence of a moſt formidably dry and parching wind. The true Bedouin Arab never ſhaves either his head or beard; and his hair, difpoſed into ten or twelve treſſes, floats careleſsly down his ſhoulders. The head-drefs of the women is almoſt the fame; and indeed one perceives very little difference between the dreſs of the two ſexes, except in the colour of the handkerchief, and the jewels employed to adorn the head of the female. The *abe* of the women, ſerves for a complete veil to the face, there being only a ſmall and neceſſary aperture for the eyes: in many parts of thefe deferts, however, the Arabs of both fexes go entirely naked.

The Bedouins, with a degree of prudence not always equally viſible in their conduct, as will afterwards appear, leaving their camels deſtined for the Aleppo market confiderably behind us, proceeded a quarter of a mile from the Arabian camp. One of our men now ran before, to requeſt the friendſhip of the tribe, a requeſt which, of courſe, is complied with almoſt as ſoon as a ſtranger has arrived within the lines of

their

their encampment. It is granted, however, according to cuftom, under all the formalities of war; and therefore a party of the Arabian warriors, rufhing inftantly from their camp, ran full fpeed towards our caravan. The Bedouins difmounted from their dromedaries, and proceeded with equal celerity to meet them, when mingling with much apparent rage, each holding his lance pointed againft the breaft of his opponent, they exhibited a mock fight, accompanied with loud fhouts on both fides. We were foon introduced to the camp, when peace and good order were immediately reftored. My companions were defirous to have fome traffic in camels, and we fojourned within the lines of the Arabian encampment two days and a half.

One day I went on a vifit to the Arabian camp entirely alone, for my conductor, either really or affecting to be afraid of fome difagreeable adventure, declined his attendance. About the diftance of forty paces from their tents I was accofted by a fingle Arab, who defired to know my bufinefs. Having made him underftand that

VOL. II. H I was

I was a ſtranger in the deſert, and that curioſity alone had led me that way, he ſaluted me with much civility, and conducting me to his tent as a mark of his hoſpitality placed me in the uppermoſt ſeat. He was by profeſſion a ſmith, and had a little furnace, which he heated with charcoal obtained from the roots of brambles gathered in the deſert; and had contrived to piece four ſkins in the form of a large bladder, which, receiving a conſtant preſſure from two of his children, ſerved in place of a bellows. This, like all the other tents in the camp, was much longer than broad, with a partition in the middle: the firſt apartment belonged to the maſter of the family, while the ſecond was occupied by his wife and other females, who were employed in dreſſing wool. I made it my buſineſs to examine the wells of the Arabs, which I found to be nothing more than large holes dug in the earth, without any lining whatever, and in which the water ſtood at the depth of ſix feet from the ſurface. One of the moſt beautiful mares I had ever ſeen was ſtanding at the door of
a neigh-

a neighbouring tent, which I likewife took
the liberty to enter. Here I was extremely
well received by a good old Arab, who was
employed in making bottles and troughs of
goat-fkins; every creature I met, even to
the mare and her foal, came to fmell me.
I proceeded to make the tour of another
circle of tents, and found them all open to
leeward, but fhut againft the burning wind
of the defert, which prevails fix months in
the fame quarter. It feemed to be the
chief employment of this little commonwealth to drefs goats hair, and the wool of
their fheep and camels. One circumftance
which furprized me not a little, was the in-
curious and indifferent air of the people,
who, though they treated me with civility,
yet never ftirred from their feats at my approach. Their tents being open lengthways, I had an opportunity of obferving
that an Arab's family is remarkably populous. This liftlefs inattention, efpecially in
children, always eager to examine whatever has the air of novelty, appeared to me
to be extremely fingular; and the more fo,
fince ftrangers are but feldom feen in this

part of Arabia, it being near the centre of the defert.

The whole property of an Arab confifts of his herds and flocks; his horfes, but more efpecially his mares, which he confiders as much more valuable, are of great ufe to him in his excurfions, and particularly in the purfuits of war: he is eminently diftinguifhed as a horfeman, and much more fkilful in the management of that animal than the native of any other country. The Arabian horfe, which feeds only once a day, and even then makes but a fcanty meal, is at the fame time the fleeteft and moft abftemious animal in the world.

The camel is perhaps of no lefs confequence to his roving mafter; he ferves to tranfport his family and property from one part of the defert to another, and is, befides, an article of traffic for grain and other neceffaries of life. When, in confequence of extreme drought, his grafs begins to fail, or his well to be dried up, the Arab decamps, and goes in queft of water and pafture in lefs inhofpitable regions. The whole defert is covered with a fine fand mixed with gravel,

gravel, which produces only a few brambles about a foot and a half high, and a kind of grafs with a fingle ftalk of four inches, but which is never found incorporated in the manner of our green turf.

CHAP. XII.

Expedients the Arab employs to fhelter himfelf, in the defert, from the fcorching winds and reflection of the fands.—Character of the Arabs.—Their police, and civil regulations.—Political confiderations upon the right of the wandering Arab to the defert he inhabits.

DURING the fummer months there prevails in the plains of Arabia a N. W. wind, violently heated by the reflection of the fand; and in winter the fcorching heat of the S. E. is perhaps ftill more infupportable. In this feafon the rays of the fun are fo powerful, that the human

H 3 fkin

skin becomes crisped, and the pores so constricted as to impede the ordinary course of perspiration. Hence the Arabian has been taught to interpose a very dense medium between his body and the solar rays, against which an European winter dress of the most substantial fabric would prove but a slender defence: he doubles down a thick handkerchief tied round the forehead, over his mouth and nose, in order to prevent that moisture which is necessary to the lungs from being entirely exhausted; he is obliged, however, to leave his eyes wholly unprotected, which suffer the most acute pain from the heat and violent reflection of the sand, and which consequently become in an early period of life greatly weakened and impaired.

As the general aspect of the desert is that of a vast plain terminated on all sides by the horizon, in vain does the roving eye of the traveller seek to rest on some intervening object; and hence, after flitting over a dismal waste of grey sand and scorched brambles, it returns at last, languid and fatigued, to enjoy a little relaxation in the variety

riety of herds and other Arabian property with which it is furrounded. A deep and mournful filence reigns over the dreary landfcape; no beaft, no bird, no fpecies of infect, is feen to diverfify the fad uniformity of the fcene. In the whole extent of Arabia Deferta I faw only four rabbits, five or fix rats, three large, and feven or eight fmall birds. The laft were, befides, in the vicinity of an inhabited country, whilft the former were natives of a more earthy foil than is eafily to be met with in thefe regions.

The fpecies of rat I have mentioned is remarkably handfome, and of a breed very different from any I had before met with: his eyes are large and fprightly; the whif-kers, fnout, and brow, as well as the belly, feet, and end of the tail, are white, whilft the other parts of the body are covered with a long neat fur of a yellow colour: the tail is rather fhort, thick, yellow, and pointed with white. Some of thefe animals were killed, and, after being roafted, eaten by the Arabs, who are accuftomed to throw their fticks with furprifing dex-

terity

terity at whatever bird or quadruped happens to come in their way.

The ſmall quantity of water found in this vaſt deſert is extremely ſalt and bitter; but the Arab is trained to the hardſhips, and attached to the freedom of his native plains. Inured to fatigue, and careleſs of the conveniencies of a wealthier ſituation, he looks down on the effeminate pleaſures of more temperate climates with ſcorn and contempt. Brave, proud, hoſpitable, and enterprizing, he is true to all his engagements. Being conſtantly expoſed, however, to the inroads of warlike tribes, he is prone to ſuſpicion, and hence receives all ſtrangers whatever with arms in his hands. The individuals of the ſame tribe, even of the loweſt condition, being regarded by the reſt of the clan in the light of brothers, any injury done to one is received and reſented as an inſult offered to the whole. They are extremely cautious of engaging in an affair from which blood may be expected to enſue; but are proportionally ſtimulated to action, in contempt

of

of every danger, when they have a cause to avenge.

The Arab is unfortunate enough to imagine that he has the same right to interfere with the property of another, which he, in exercising the offices of hospitality with regard to his own, parts with to a stranger, and in this sense may be said to be a robber; but in no case can he be charged nationally with the character of an assassin. From the combination of these virtues and prejudices, seem to result the strength and union of the Arabian tribes; and were their manners a little more humanized by the influence of Christian morality, I know no race of men whose character would bid fairer for happiness, or be less liable to exception. The extreme barrenness of their deserts, which discourages the ambition, and defends them against the yoke, of a conqueror, the certainty of subsistence, and the total exclusion of luxury, constitute their great charter to independance, and those undepraved and simple manners, by which they have always been distinguished.

His

His strong attachment to freedom makes an Arab cautious of acknowledging any authority in his chief, which he cannot discover to be expedient for the good of the community; but at the same time, being frequently at war with his neighbours, he is sensible that there must be one man, in whose discretion on such occasions the national will ought to center, in order that the tribe may take the field in a body, and act with proper effect against the enemy. The Arabian tribes in general bear the name of the primitive stock whence they are respectively descended, and have no other appellation than that of his children; the Arabs by whom I was accompanied were called Ben Halet, or the children of Halet.

The Arabs run with extraordinary swiftness, and are singularly dexterous in the management of the lance, have large bones, a deep brown complexion, persons of an ordinary stature, but lean, muscular, active, and vigorous. The Bedouins suffer their hair and beards to grow; and, indeed, among the Arabian tribes in general, the beard

beard is remarkably full and bufhy. The
Arab has a large ardent black eye, a long
face, features high and regular, and, as the
refult of the whole, a phyfiognomy particularly ftern and fevere. This marked expreffion, meeting with our pre-conceived
notions of his character, gives him an air
of great ferocity; upon a little acquaintance, however, his formidable afpect fettles into fomething truly noble and manly.

The tribes which frequent the middle
of the defert have locks fomewhat crifped,
extremely fine, and approaching the woolly
hair of the negro: my own, during the
fhort period of my travels in thefe regions,
became more dry and delicate than ufual,
and, receiving little nourifhment from a
checked perfpiration, fhewed a difpofition
to affume the fame frizzled and woolly
appearance. An entire failure of moifture,
and the exceffive heat of climate by which
it was occafioned, feemed to be the principal caufes of thefe fymptoms; my blood
was become extremely dry, and my complection differed little at laft from that of
a Hindoo or Arab. It is not my intention,
however,

however, to offer any theory relative to the strong influence climate may be suppofed to have on the external appearance of the human frame.

Having confidered the Arab with much attention as to his manners and principles of action, I cannot agree in the common opinion which makes a propenfity to robbery a natural ingredient in his character. I had the ftrongeft evidence, in various fituations, of the honefty and fidelity of my fellow-travellers: I faw them as a little commonwealth living on the moft friendly and fociable terms; nor, indeed, have I ever heard that an Arab would be guilty of theft or robbery againft thofe of his own tribe. His appetite for plunder is exerted, in concert with his clan, againft ftrangers, and always within the boundaries of the deferts. In no fhape whatever will an Arab invade the property of another man in a town or cultivated country; and hence robbery in him is plainly derived from a prejudice of education, a prejudice in all refpects fimilar to that of the ancient Romans, who regarded every tribe and race of men not in their alliance, as enemies of the republic.

The Arab pays a fcrupulous regard to all his engagements with ftrangers; and therefore the traveller, upon making a certain gratification, in confideration of being fuffered to pafs unmolefted, or upon receiving the protection of any individual Arab, who, in this cafe, from their fraternal union, is conceived to reprefent the tribe, enjoys an entire exemption from the ordinary effects of Arabian prejudices againft ftrangers. In fuch circumftances, a foreigner may crofs the deferts with as little apprehenfion of injuftice from the natives, as he ever entertained in travelling a high road in his native country.

That the Arab's right to his deferts is of a lefs perfect kind than that of other nations to the countries they refpectively inhabit, is an argument that will hardly be maintained; fince, if long and uninterrupted poffeffion, agreeably to the legal maxims of every civilized people, founds the requifites of dominion, it is evident that his claim to the deferts is much lefs liable to exception

than

than that of any prince whatever to the domains of his crown. But is there a sovereign or independent ſtate in the world which does not vindicate an excluſive right to all the uſes of its ſoil?—or is this a rule of juriſprudence, in which the Arab alone is excepted?—a prince deſtitute of authority even on his own eſtate, and who muſt patiently give way to ſtrangers paſſing at diſcretion over his grounds? To this right of abſolute dominion, however, he has never rigidly adhered; all he requires is a certain tribute or cuſtom, proportioned to the quantity of goods or merchandize meant to be tranſported over the deſerts; a cuſtom, beſides, which every individual of the tribe, as repreſenting the community, has authority to exact or diſpenſe with at his diſcretion.

This privilege, veſted in every member of the clan, is of general notoriety; and therefore intelligent travellers take care to have an Arab in their company, for a pledge of peace and ſecurity againſt the moleſtation of his tribe.

Such is the political conſtitution of the
deſert,

desert, and whoever conducts himself in conformity to it has nothing to dread from the depredations of the natives. But if men, acting from ignorance, or in contempt of Arabian manners, expose themselves to be pillaged, they have no right to represent the Arabs collectively, and without distinction or enquiry, in the odious colours of robbers and banditti.

The peculiar circumstances of this country must, no doubt, often render his life personally painful to the native; but his hardships are considerably counterbalanced by the sweets of independence, and that confidence and affection which unite him to his tribe in all its interests and pursuits.

CHAP.

CHAP. XIII.

Contrast betwixt the simple Arab, and the inhabitant of a refined country.—Amusements and employments of the natives of the desert.—The march of a tribe of Arabs across the desert described.—The caravan of shepherds resumes its journey.—And the Author describes a very picturesque scene in the desert.

I MUST own I never felt so sensibly as in the desert, and in the wilds of America, the charms of that invaluable liberty which is the gift of the Creator, but which in great cities and highly civilized countries is almost extinguished by the habits of luxury, and the miserable restraints of idle and artificial distinctions. A rude mantle, which he carries constantly about with him, serves to defend the Arab and his family against the oppressive heat of the sun, as well as the inconveniencies of rain; his robe, larger in size, but in the style of that of St. John the

the Baptist, woven with his own hands, which never felt the edge of the scissars, and which he consequently owes to his own industry alone, is all the cloathing he requires. If he looks around him, the soil, as far as he can see, is his own, while at the same time he affects neither land-mark nor inclosure, but shares with his Arabian kindred the pasture of his flocks. He goes wherever he chooses, and nothing impedes his steps; but had he been born in a polished country, every joint of his body would have been cramped and embarrassed with ligaments of twenty different kinds, the acquisition of which would have cost him much pain and anxiety, while the enjoyment of them could only flatter a mind of the weakest vanity. In fine, he would have found it difficult to turn himself to the right hand or to the left, without infringing on some custom or punctilio, equally inconsistent, perhaps, with the maxims of good sense and the natural order of things.

The freedom and equality of condition enjoyed by the natives, in spite of the dismal aspect of their deserts, created in my mind

mind many emotions of inftinctive pleafure; an admonition which I confider as the voice of nature, and whence I am inclined to infer the real value and importance of thefe advantages. The circumftances of the Arab by no means preclude him from the enjoyment of pleafure; befides an habitual and animating fenfe of his independance, he drinks the milk of his cattle, and regales himfelf with many palatable difhes to which we are ftrangers: he runs and dances with great vivacity, and practifes many other manly and ufeful exercifes. His dances are fometimes gay and exhilarating, but he is more particularly addicted to fuch as are warlike, and have a tendency to train him for the day of battle; in thefe the Arab goes through various evolutions, his lance in his hand, with the moft dexterous agility. Thefe dances are equally in ufe among the Biffayan and Javanefe Indians, with this difference only, that the latter are armed with the buckler as well as the lance. The dances more peculiar to the women are of two kinds, the one fprightly and gay, the other impaffioned and voluptuous,

tuous, the object of which is to excite certain ideas in a manner extremely expreffive. As in thefe it is the principal intention that the ruling fentiment be ftrongly marked in the eye, and the expreffion of the features be in harmony with the motions and attitudes of the body, it is neceffary to the dancer's performing with approbation, that her imagination be highly inflamed. Of this fpecies of dance, the Spanifh fandango, and the calenda of America, afford a faint reprefentation; and it is probable the Spaniards, as well as the negroes of Guinea and Angola, borrowed it from the Arabians.

Their wool, the ftaple commodity of the deferts, ferves as the materials of the cloth and tapeftry of the Arabs; and thefe would by no means difgrace the dexterity of an European manufacturer. Of their goat-fkins they make bottles and troughs for giving water to their cattle. Their flocks, which, on account of their rapid increafe, would foon become a burthen to their owners, they barter in civilized countries for articles of drefs, corn, dates, and whatever elfe their neceffities require. Such of the Arabian

bian tribes as border on the Euphrates and improveable lands, cultivate a small portion of ground; but as soon as the seed-time is over they betake themselves to the roving pursuits of the desert, and only return in autumn, in order to reap the benefit of the harvest.

A tribe of Arabs on their march across the desert is a very curious and entertaining object. On this occasion a vast extent of plain presents itself to the eye, covered with herds and flocks, preceded by a troop of camels laden with tents, baggage, and poultry, animals which, at the first signal for their departure, instantly take wing and perch on the back of the dromedary. Behind these is another set of camels, charged with all the lame and infirm animals, which, by their various and discordant cries, give sufficient notice of the pain and hardships of their confinement. Upon a third set are groupes of women and children, whose painful screams mix in strange confusion with the bleating and bellowing of numberless animals, of all humours, ages, and species. It is difficult to conceive a more

irksome

irkfome fituation than that of the Arab's wife, in the midft of her children, weeping, fighting, and fcrambling all around her. Such of the women as are exempt from the incumbrance of infants, employ themfelves on their camels in fpinning, or grinding corn with hand-mills. High above this fingular mafs of tumult and diforder, appears a foreft of lances, at leaft eight or ten feet in length, while the ear is ftunned with the hoarfe voice of the Arab, chiding, expoftulating, or commanding filence in his family; but whofe chief care is to form a ftrong rampart for the defence of the little commonwealth on its march.

It was the intention of the Bedouins to have purfued their route through the middle of the defert; and this, by drawing us to a diftance from the Arabian encampments, feemed to promife fecurity againft all moleftation from the natives. But it being reprefented by the Arabs of this camp, that, among other inconveniencies refulting from fuch a ftep, we fhould not find a drop of water, either for ourfelves or camels, we determined to direct our

courfe

course towards the banks of the Euphrates. Next day, therefore, we proceeded to lay in a stock of water at the wells of the adjacent camp; and on this occasion I had a second opportunity of observing the phlegmatic inattention of the Arabs. If at any time they quitted their tents, it was not to observe the appearance of us strangers, but to milk their cattle, which by the bye is the business of the women, or for the management of other domestic concerns. We filled our bottles with the same tranquillity as if we had been in the heart of the desert; and I particularly remarked, that although I was the only individual, at this time, who was mounted on a camel, and was pointed out to their attention by some peculiarities of dress, I could only attract the notice of two or three children. Some of the tribe were at the well, employed like ourselves in filling their bottles, some in conducting their flocks to pasture in the vicinity, and some, after having milked their goats, called the family to breakfast with the same apathy and indifference as if they had been entirely by themselves. If our presence had any effect

at

at all, it was upon the minds of the women, who ufed to cover a fmall part of the face upon appearing without their tents.

As foon as we were provided with water, we refumed our journey, keeping a little more to the N. E.; and, after travelling four days, came to a deferted caftle with three towers, on the confines of a fmall lake. Here we were under the neceffity of again filling our bottles, though the water was of a nature extremely difagreeable both to the fmell and tafte. Meanwhile thirft, as well as curiofity, drew me towards the caftle and its lake; and I foon faw, what is an object of great rarity in thofe regions, a piece of water covered with bulrufhes waving in the wind. It is impoffible for me to defcribe the emotions of joy occafioned by this profpect; fuffice it to fay, that I approached it with great alacrity; but how great was my difappointment, when, inftead of the enchanting fpot my imagination had fuggefted, I met with a piece of moift marfhy ground, which contained water of all the colours of the rainbow, corrupting in the fun, and every where

emitting a moſt peſtilential odour! I made
ſhift to penetrate where it ſeemed to be of
the greateſt depth, in hopes I ſhould find
water there of a leſs offenſive quality; but
even here the water was extremely diſco-
loured, and the adjoining reeds appearing
to have acquired its diſmal hue, my ſtomach
revolted at the idea of raiſing it to my lips.
My tongue, however, was parched with the
burning wind of the deſert, and I was im-
pelled to drink: ſuch, however, was the
fœtid taſte of this ſtagnated pool, that I was
able to gulp down one mouthful of it only;
and I retired, with little gratification either
to my thirſt or curioſity. The caſtle ſtands
cloſe to the lake, on a mound of earth probably artificial. I made it my buſineſs to
get within the wall; but the door was ſo
extremely ſmall, it being only two feet and
a half high, and not more than one half of
this dimenſion in breadth, that I can ſcarcely
ſuppoſe it had ever been intended for common uſe. The wall was built of earth, and
of conſiderable thickneſs. Having with
ſome difficulty made my way into this ſin-
gular building, I found a large ſquare, in
three

three corners of which were three towers, whose doors were still on a smaller scale than the one by which I had entered. I at length, however, got to the top, and observed from one of the towers, that, instead of a parapet, the artist had inclined the wall in such a manner, that one might discover any object at the foot of the castle. He had likewise given the curtain between the towers a curved form, in order, no doubt, to facilitate the means of its defence. Having satisfied my curiosity as to the nature of a building so little expected in the desert, I began to open my eyes to a view of the surrounding country; and here all my ideas of the Arabian deserts, such as they may be found in the poetical language of Oriental tales, were short of the truth. A stillness, like the silence of night; the faint remains of a breeze, still glowing with the fervour of the meridian sun, but now sinking with his orb; around, an unbounded waste, covered with a dark grey sand, resembling the ashes of a furnace, and according with the raging heat of these regions; the vast canopy of the heavens,

across

acrofs whofe pale atmofphere no object was feen but the reddifh difk of the fun dipt in the horizon, in the moment of his departure,—were a few of thofe interefting objects which confpired, on this occafion, to imprefs my mind with an unpleafing melancholy. I defcended from the caftle, and proceeded to join my companions.

CHAP. XIV.

The author's companions make an unprovoked attack upon a few Arabs—they are furprized, in confequence, by a large body of Arabian horfe and foot.—Several fkirmifhes enfue, in which the caravan is worfted by the Arabs.—The author, in his fubfequent flight, fuffers almoft inexpreffible hardfhips, and lofes his baggage, his money, and his provifions.

WE purfued our route in the fame direction, and in two days came to fome wells, contiguous to four tents, the
women

women belonging to which gave us their affiftance in mending and filling our bottles. Next morning I very narrowly efcaped diflocating my neck by a fall from my camel, as he got up to refume his march.

In a further progrefs of three days we defcried, towards evening, twelve Arabs in the defert, with a company of camels. The chief of our caravan, tempted, I apprehend, by the fmallnefs of their number, having ordered his men to give chace, they were purfued and fired upon : in their flight they left behind them fome linen, bottles, and clubs. I was by no means fatisfied with this atchievement of the Bedouins; and, thinking it very improbable that thefe men perambulated the defert by themfelves, dreaded the confequences of fo unprovoked an act of hoftility. I compared the late extreme caution with which I had feen our people approach the lines of an Arabian camp, with this wanton bravado of courage againft a handful of men deftitute of arms ; and fecretly condemned the conduct of the caravan.

We

We paffed the enfuing night, however, without moleftation, and, early next morning, refumed our journey; but about noon, the apprehenfions I had entertained the evening before began to be realized; for all of a fudden we faw a body of men on horfeback, riding towards us at full fpeed. The Bedouins ftooped their camels, and entered into a conference with a meffenger who came to treat with us on the part of the enemy. It was but too evident, however, that they could come to no agreement; for the Arab returned to his friends, and the people of our caravan ran inftantly to arms.

Meanwhile we continued our march; but, after an interval of little more than a quarter of an hour, we obferved a large body of horfe and foot in purfuit of us. We again ftooped our camels as compactly as poffible, at the fame time difplaying a flag, containing certain figures and characters in white upon a blue ground. Our mufketeers, advancing about two hundred paces, pofted themfelves in the front of the caravan. The lances halted at the diftance of fifty paces before the Bedouin ftandard, which

which was erected at the corner of the camp, on the side of the enemy, and defended by the rest of the Bedouins, armed chiefly with clubs and sabres. The Arabs advanced in order of battle, to the number of five hundred men, while our whole force consisted only of a hundred and fifty. The Bedouins, however, waited their approach with steadiness and resolution, shouting " Allah-ou-Allah!" which I understood to be an invocation of God to witness the justice of their cause, and to succour them in battle. The enemy having approached within two hundred paces of our musketeers, began a kind of running fight, such as I had seen practised in the Arabian camp, which I have already had frequent occasion to mention. The Bedouins kept up an irregular fire upon their opponents; when the Arabs, extending themselves as if they had meant to surround us, chose to decline a close engagement, and were contented with discharging their pieces against the caravan. When at any time, however, they seemed desirous of closing with the Bedouins, we rose in a body, and advanced

vanced full speed to meet them; while they, as it should seem, perceiving we were prepared for the conflict, retreated slowly on the plain.

The engagement continued to be maintained in this indecisive manner, till the approach of night, when the main body of the enemy having retired to a considerable distance from the caravan, the musketeers drew nearer to each other. On our side there was not one man killed or wounded, while the Bedouins boasted of having killed three or four men and two camels belonging to the Arabs. We kept, during the night, a picquet towards the enemy, as well as a rear-guard, which was more immediately charged with the safety of the caravan. The close attention given by both parties to the signal or watch-word, which was repeated in very extraordinary cries, suggested no mean idea of their military conduct and circumspection. Now all was joy and uproar in the Bedouin camp; and our warriors, elated with the success of the preceding day, celebrated the victory by dances descriptive of all the manœuvres of

an

an Arabian battle. While it was their
bufinefs to ftimulate the national courage
of the tribe, by the frequent repetition of
" Ben Halet," they were equally anxious
to excite their whole rage againft their opponents, by the moft violent exclamations
of " Turkis," or " Turk," which fignifies,
in their acceptation of the word, an impla-
cable enemy. I took the liberty to obferve
to my conductor, who feemed to be a fenfible as well as brave man, that a little repofe would, in my opinion, be a better pre-
parative for a new engagement in the morning, than thofe intemperate and unfeafon-
able gufts of joy; and likewife, that, without waiting till the Arabs fhould be ftrength-
ened by the arrival of any additional force,
we ought to refume our march by day-
break, placing our camels in the center,
and our armed men on the two wings, who
might be in conftant readinefs to repel the
attacks of the enemy. My advice was little regarded, and I was not fufficiently acquainted with the Arabic language to deliver my opinion in a council of war,
which was now fitting round the Bedouin
§ ftandard.

standard. I committed myself, therefore, to the care of Providence, and resolved to profit by a small interval of repose: this was, however, interrupted by the balls of the Arabs, which at times whistled about my ears.

The engagement was renewed early in the morning; and, after lasting two hours, similar in all respects to that of the preceding day, the combatants on both sides withdrew from the field. The caravan had a second conference with the enemy; and at eight o'clock I received a message from the Bedouins, desiring me to deliver to them all the money in my possession; with which requisition I very readily complied. Couriers, however, were continually arriving as before, and, as I heard no farther mention of the money, probably intended for our ransom, I concluded that every idea of reconcilement between the contending parties was abandoned. Accordingly I soon learned, that the enemy would accept of nothing less than the plunder of the whole caravan; and that, to complete this unfortunate adventure, we were now wholly at

their

their difcretion. I am convinced, however, that fo great an animofity to a caravan, which, according to cuftom immemorial, is conftantly permitted, for a certain acknowledgment in money, to proceed without difturbance, could only be owing to our wanton attack of the twelve Arabs, aggravated, perhaps, by fome effufion of blood in the firft engagement. Upon receiving a final anfwer from the enemy, we again ftood to our arms, though confcious we were far from being in a condition to hold out for any length of time againft the hardfhips of our prefent fituation. It was now five days fince we laft filled our bottles, and our water was nearly exhaufted. The exceffive heat and conftant fatigue and agitation of body and mind, to which we had for a confiderable time been expofed, had, befides, nearly exhaufted our ftrength.

Towards evening the Arabs made a feint to renew the attack, but they declined approaching nearer to us than within the diftance of a gun-fhot, and we had not one man either killed or wounded. Night coming on, the enemy retired to the diftance of half a league on the plain; when we took care, as before, to post an advanced guard, which, with sentinels stationed on all sides of the caravan, watched the motions of the enemy. Having observed that our men, after lighting a great many fires in the camp, formed themselves into small circles, and whispered each other, I conjectured that some sudden and secret enterprize was in agitation : and accordingly, about ten o'clock, they began to saddle their camels, and my conductor desired me to give him my linen, that he might pack it up with his own. Another Bedouin, having charged himself with the least weighty part of my provisions, advised me to abandon the remainder. I saw the whole caravan employed in a similar manner; and, every thing being concerted and ready, I was exhorted to be on my guard, and above all things to stick fast to my dromedary, for that in a few moments the caravan would betake itself to flight.

What a dismal prospect was now before me! I was to follow the caravan at the dreadful gallop of the camel; the hard step and stubborn nature of which must expose me every instant to the most alarming accidents. If unfortunately I should happen to fall at the first outset, I must either be crushed to death by my companions, or be left alone a prey to all the miseries of the desert. In this case my only chance of safety would have been, by taking a northern course, to have endeavoured to reach the banks of the Euphrates, which at this season are frequented by Arabian tribes; but which were distant at least four days journey. There were moments when I could not help secretly wishing the enemy to overtake us, being satisfied I had now nothing more desirable to expect, than either to perish by the sword, or to surrender myself a prisoner. But I had been informed that the Arabs were accustomed to give no quarter to their enemies, even after plundering them; considering themselves bound by the ties of hospitality only within the lines of their tents, which were probably at a great distance. I resigned myself, therefore, to the disposal of Divine Providence, and, having seated myself firmly on my bolsters, expected patiently the signal for flight.

About four o'clock in the morning we set up the usual cry, *Bonne garde?* or, Who goes there? while at the same time the Bedouins were busily employed, all over the camp, in lighting up fires, which, as they were only kept alive by a sort of withered bramble gleaned in the desert, were of very short duration. This stratagem was succeeded by an interval of dead silence; when at length, at half an hour after four, as the advanced guard was still hallooing *Bonne garde?* my good Arab came to see if I was properly seated on my camel, and in the same instant the whole caravan shot over the desert, like a flash of lightning, into the S. W.

Across an amazing cloud of dust, occasioned by the abrupt manner of our departure, and which must have been terrible to a spectator at a distance, I began to observe that the young camels, intended for sale, had each a fetter on one of his feet; a precaution which was meant to free us of their incumbrance, as well as to obstruct

the

the progrefs of the Arabs, by diverting their attention from the principal object of their purfuit. We fled three leagues towards the fouth, at the full ftretch of the dromedary; in the courfe of which I fat perched as upon a table; and nothing but the hand of Providence could have prevented my falling from the back of this animal, whofe motions were fo intolerably fevere, that at every ftep my bowels feemed to be fhaken in pieces. My hands, one holding faft before and the other behind, fupported me like a kind of buttrefs, by which means they were much bruifed and lacerated, while my nerves had loft their fpring and fenfibility in fo great a degree, that I was twenty times on the point of abandoning my hold.

Meanwhile the enemy were in clofe purfuit of us; but a part of our caravan having fallen into their hands, they loft fome time in pillaging the effects and catching the young camels; and on this occafion my poor Arabian cook, whom I hired at Baffora, had the misfortune to be among the number of the captives. The enemy, how-

however, being occupied with their plunder, gave us time to leave them considerably behind; and therefore, after running three leagues further S. E. our little troop, which by this time confisted of seven persons only, resolved to detach itself intirely from the remains of the caravan. What was the fate of the other Arabs, I cannot pretend to say, having never, from that moment, received the smallest intelligence concerning them. We made a large circuit round the region which we had just traversed, and thus, by leaving our pursuers, and the rest of the caravan, to prosecute a route directly contrary to ours, we resumed our former direction towards the N. W.

Having continued our flight in this direction with the same celerity, we at length came to a district of the desert covered with large stones and fragments of rocks; and here my camel stumbling against a stone, and at the same instant making a jerk to one side of the path, I lost my hold, and was thrown off to some distance; but happily a good Arab was at hand, who immediately stooped his camel, and took me ine up behind him; my dromedary, mean time, having taken flight, overturned his baggage, and a Bedouin cutting the ropes, I was deprived at once of all my provisions, with a confiderable part of my other ne- ceffaries, while my camel went unloaded before us.

CHAP. XV.

The Author and his companions efcape from the Arabs their purfuers.—Friendly at- tentions of the Bedouin fhepherds.—A frefh alarm renews the Author's fufferings.— Defcription of the Arabian dromedary.

ABOUT eight o'clock we entered the dry bed of a torrent, and were at pains to conceal ourfelves, whilft one of our men went to reconnoitre from an emi- nence what was paffing in the plain. He could difcover neither the enemy nor the caravan, and we again mounted our camels; but I was now feated on a miferable pack- faddle, saddle, confifting of a rude bolfter of hay placed round the dromedary's bunch, with four pieces of a board imitating the ftock of a faddle. As we rode nearly with the fame difpatch we had employed before, my fufferings are not to be defcribed.

At ten, in the vicinity of a rock, we difcovered a fpring of fweet water furrounded with fhrubs, a circumftance which feemed to announce its good quality. Completely worn out with thirft and fatigue, I was unable to reftrain the importunity of nature, and took almoft a bottle of it at one draught; but I foon became indifpofed, and had reafon to be forry for the imprudence of my conduct. If we had had any fufpicion of meeting the enemy in this quarter, the recent traces of cattle which had been watering in the morning would have increafed our apprehenfions. We took care, however, to place a fentinel on a rifing ground, who kept a fharp lookout, while we remained in readinefs to continue our flight at the firft fignal. As he could difcover neither man nor beaft in the wide extent of the defert, we were fatisfied

fied that by our counter-march we had entirely efcaped the obfervation of the Arabs.

I now confidered in what manner I could reward my friend the Arab, who fo generoufly ftooped his dromedary, and took me up, when I had the misfortune to fall from my own. I could not fail to reflect that while he delivered me from immediate death, or perhaps from the more deplorable calamity of ftarving in the defert, he had expofed himfelf to the imminent danger of falling into the hands of an enraged enemy: My money was reduced to the very trifling fum of four piaftres, which, with an earneft requeft that he would accept of them as a fmall teftimony of affectionate gratitude, I prefented to my benefactor. So familiar, however, are the fentiments of charity and beneficence in the minds of thefe people, that he had no idea of what prompted me to offer him money. Upon his modeft but peremptory refufal, I laid the pieces on his robe, and left him. In a few minutes, however, he came to me with the money in his hand; and fuch was the delicacy of this worthy man's feelings, that he was not perfuaded suaded into compliance, until I had assured him that I offered these piastres, not as the reward of his services, but as the memorial of a friend, who loved and esteemed him.

I had now no provisions of my own, having lost them in the desert; but I had little cause of regret, as the good Arabs took care to administer to my wants. They baked oaten cakes, and toasted them on the sand, or at a fire of brambles, and having spread them with dates, or butter obtained from the milk of the female camel, applied them a second time to the heat. At our meals I was constantly treated with a larger portion of this buttered cake, which is far from being a bad ragout, than fell to the share of any of my companions. In consequence, however, of the great diminution of our provisions, it was but seldom we could afford this treat, and were obliged to have recourse to dates as our chief means of subsistence. This singular attention in the Bedouins, which was above the suspicion of an interested motive, continued to be exercised towards me in the same manner and degree to the day of our separation.

Our

Our fears of the enemy, which were greatly encreafed by frefh traces of cattle vifible about the well, not permitting us to linger, after dinner we mounted our camels, and fled till night, almoft with the fame rapidity as in the morning. My pain and fatigue were fcarcely to be borne; every inch of my feat applied to the pack-faddle was covered with fores; and, partly owing to my infirmities, and partly to the loofe condition of the faddle, which was thrown backwards at every ftep of the dromedary, I was frequently pitched upon his hump. My nerves were benumbed, and become incapable of farther exertions, while my fingers, in confequence of an extreme agitation in my blood, fhook involuntarily, like the keys of a harpfichord. In this miferable condition I loft my appetite, and was unable to take the nourifhment neceffary to my fupport; but I looked forward with hope of relief to that refrefhing repofe I promifed myfelf during the approaching night. About nine o'clock in the evening, however, I was told by the Arabs that it was neceffary to go on. There was

was no time left to expoſtulate; I mounted my dromedary in the beſt manner I was able, and went on at a long ſtep, which I endeavoured to bear with all the fortitude in my power.

At two o'clock in the morning we halted at a piece of hollow ground, where we lay down and ſlept till ſix. We again mounted our camels, and purſued our journey the whole day, ſometimes at a trot, ſometimes at a kind of gallop, according as the deſert ſeemed more or leſs frequented. The following morning we diſcovered the banks of the Euphrates, on which ſtood a ſolitary building; but having ſuddenly obſerved a company of Arabs, we turned the heads of our camels, and fled full ſpeed. We paſſed heaps of ſtones at different intervals, which were probably deſigned for a direction of the road. I obſerved likewiſe large mounds of earth, but whether natural or artificial I cannot pretend to ſay. In regulating our flight, we were directed by the N. W. wind in the day-time, and at night took our direction from the motions of the ſtars.

The

The Arabian dromedary, which differs from that of Africa, being fmaller, and having but one bunch, feems to be particularly intended for the ufe of man in thefe defert regions. Notwithftanding the extreme fatigue to which the dromedary I rode was fubjected in confequence of very long ftages, and although he was occafionally four or five days without water, eating only a few brambles, which he gleaned in the defert in the hurry of his march, he appeared to have no complaint. He remained, befides, ftooped, according to cuftom, during the whole courfe of the night. The dromedary is endowed with the faculty of bringing up his food, which he fwallows at firft in hafte, and which he ruminates afterwards at his convenience, in the manner of the ox. It is unneceffary for me to defcribe the ftructure of an animal fo univerfally known.

Our difcovery at this moment of a well was a fortunate event, as our bottles were almoft entirely empty; but, finding it expedient to fpend little time in taking a fupply of water, we

we departed as we had arrived, at full
speed, in order to elude the keepers of cattle, whose traces were observable all around
the well.

CHAP. XVI.

*The company reach several high mountains,
which announce their being on the border
of the desert.—After various alarms and
difficulties, they at length meet with a village, situated in a cultivated country.*

IN four days we saw a ridge of high
mountains on the left, stretching along
the horizon; and a little afterwards there
appeared a small cloud, followed by several
others, which, as the desert had hitherto
presented a sky uniformly serene, was become an object of some curiosity.

We were still, however, subjected to
unremitting anxiety and fatigue, from the
marches and counter-marches we were

obliged

obliged to make as often as we difcovered the traces of a camel, or the footfteps of an Arab. As the little bottoms in the defert are much frequented by the natives in the fummer feafon, it often happened that, in order to avoid being difcovered after reaching the top of an eminence, we found it expedient to turn, and defcend it at full fpeed. When, as was often the cafe, our march lay through a narrow and difficult paffage, we made it our bufinefs to hide ourfelves during the day, and refumed our journey at the approach of night.

We now began to draw near to the high mountains above mentioned, when I obferved the little vallies in their vicinity white with falt-petre, which had no doubt been wafhed down from the heights, and depofited by the winter rains. In fome places the foil, formed into a dry cruft, was raifed about four inches above the level of the folid ground; infomuch that our camels, under whofe feet it broke at every ftep, found it extremely difficult to proceed. This uncommon puffed ftate of the

the foil is evidently occafioned by the exceffive heat of the fun, which prevails at the clofe of the rainy feafon.

My fellow-travellers were at pains to direct my eye to a town fituated among thefe mountains, the name of which I have forgotten, and which I was unable to defcry. I faw an Arabian fair in the plain, and paffed fome ancient ruins, which, however, from their fize, did not feem to merit much of the traveller's attention.

We met with the veftiges of encampments, which, in the winter feafon, the Arab pitches upon the heights, and generally in the vicinity of a torrent. Here the foil is of greater depth, but, on account of numberlefs rat-holes, which are probably abandoned as foon as the drought commences, is extremely painful to the feet of the camel. The earth being completely undermined, the moment the animal fets his foot on the ground, the cruft gives way, and it is not without a confiderable effort that he can extricate his hoof from the foil. Happily, however, in this embarraffing fituation we were not under the

neceffity

neceffity of travelling with our ufual expedition.

We turned to the right, and, directing our march in the line of the mountains, arrived at a watering-place in the midft of a plain. We defcended into a very deep cavern, formed by huge rocks, where we found in a vaft bafon or cavity a fountain of bitter water, which, confidering its tafte, fmell, colour, and fituation, merits a place in the catalogue of the infernal fources. Next day, at fome diftance from this cave, we lay concealed in the hollows, and as foon as it was dark refumed our journey along the fide of the hills. We had the benefit of the moon till ten, when we ftopped, and waited her going down; for, as we were about to enter a long and narrow defile, with a view to be more in the direction of Aleppo, we were afraid of falling in with the natives. Having lately feen an Arabian fair in the plain, and as we had obferved in the courfe of the day that this confined paffage, as well as the adjacent grounds, were frequented by Arabs, the apprehenfions of my fellow-travellers were

were far from appearing extravagant. We sent a scout before, to reconnoitre, and stole on without uttering a single word; for, from the dead stillness which reigns over the face of the desert, a very small noise may be heard at a considerable distance. Even our camels, whose instincts are truly wonderful, seemed to conduct themselves under similar impressions. At midnight I heard the sound of a bell in the desert, and soon after observed some Arabs belonging to a neighbouring camp, leading an ass. Dreading the consequences of being discovered, we lay down behind our camels, not without apprehending, however, that the noise of the Arabs might put our animals to flight. Fortunately they remained quiet, and our scout returned in a little time from taking a view of the country; but as we were in a state of uncertainty whether we had not been discovered by the Arabs who had just passed us, and as it was the opinion of our spy, that it would be extremely dangerous to hazard the passage under the present circumstances, we mount-. ed ed our camels in profound filence, and betook ourfelves to flight.

Continuing our route in the line of the fame mountains, we afcended them the next day; but had no fooner reached the top of the firft ridge, than, looking back upon the plain, we faw it crouded with Arabian camps, and could not help congratulating ourfelves on our fortunate efcape. Thefe are the firft heights of any confequence we had met with fince our departure from Baffora. The foil now began to be a little more fufceptible of culture, and the brambles feemed of a different fpecies from thofe of the defert. We faw a wild-boar turn into the recefs of a mountain. Upon defcending we entered a vaft plain, with diftant hills on each fide. Our profpects had now loft a great deal of their former dreary uniformity. Although I was in fome degree recovered from my firft fatigue, and a little more accuftomed to my fituation, the rude motion of the dromedary was ftill extremely painful. I cannot impute my bad plight however, to any particular delicacy of confti-
tution,

tution, fince one of the hardy Bedouins frequently lagged behind, and appeared to be at leaſt equally worn out with myſelf. In our flight over the defert I laboured under one great and peculiar difadvantage, I mean my inability to keep the camel to his proper pace; for thoſe who are uſed to travel on this animal feldom go at a trot, but almoſt always at a kind of amble, which is equally expeditious, and much leſs fevere to the rider. As this animal is actuated by a furpriſing emulation to paſs his companions on the road, when I happened to have the misfortune to be left behind, his impatience to come up with them made him conſtantly fall into a moſt formidable trot, which, it was by no means in my power either to moderate or prevent.

We filled our bottles at a well of excellent water, fituated in a kind of yard, and furrounded by the ruins of a confiderable caſtle; but obſerving the ground ſtill moiſt with water that had been recently drawn, we thought it adviſeable to fpend but little time in this place. We continued our journey, with the mountains always on the right,

right, sleeping still in the hollows during night. Next day we travelled in the same direction, permitting our camels to graze at intervals among the rocks which covered us from the obfervation of the natives. At night we proceeded along a path formed in the channel of a torrent, which we quitted in the morning to purfue our march in the direction of the mountains.

Here the footfteps of camels became very obfervable, while the defert began to be beaten, and to have the appearance of being much more frequented. Even in this place we were obliged to pafs the day as ufual, fkulking in the dry bed of a torrent, and continuing our journey during the night by the foot of the mountains.

At eight o'clock I obferved a fire on the heights, and heard the barking of dogs, by whom we had probably been perceived in the defert; fymptoms of population, which were foon confirmed by evident veftiges of the plough. At twelve we croffed feveral cultivated fields, feparated from one another by fmall ditches. At one o'clock in the morning we came to houfes, and

and a brook of running water, for the first time since we left the confines of Baſſora; and having at length entered a built village, we ſtooped our dromedaries, and ſtood to our arms. Every ſoul in the village ſeemed to be aſleep, and I was not a little inclined to follow their example.

The return of day preſented us with a country watered by rain and dew, and in no mean ſtate of improvement, embelliſhed with a number of poplars, the firſt tree I had obſerved after ſetting foot on the deſert. The villagers, intimidated by our warlike appearance, and probably miſtaking us for a band of robbers who had lately committed depredations in the wilderneſs, came to requeſt that we would withdraw into an adjacent field, where we ſhould be at liberty to refreſh ourſelves unmoleſted. We ſubmitted, and having reſted till eleven, again mounted our camels, and continued our journey in the direction of a country which appeared ſtill more beautiful and populous.

CHAP. XVII.

The scene improves upon the Author and his companions, who are agreeably surprized at finding themselves freed from any further molestation from the Arabs.—They enter Turkey, and after passing several populous villages, reach Damascus.

I WAS much entertained by the great consternation which a most complete change in the appearance of surrounding objects produced in our camels. The different aspect of a Turk and an Arab in dress, figure, and stature; the novelty of houses, dogs, trees, and rivulets; in short, every thing occurred in its turn as a cause of dismay; a circumstance which was attended with fresh difficulties to the traveller, though of a very different nature from those he had lately experienced. Our animals continued to advance with unabating diffidence and trepidation; and, on one occasion, a rat happening to run across the road,

road, threw our whole troop into terror and confufion. One of our men was difmounted, and it was not without much difficulty that the reft of the company were able to keep their feats. At the entrance to the firft bridge, the dromedary, apprehending, perhaps from the found of his feet, fome want of folidity below, made a dead paufe; and a confiderable fpace of time elapfed before we could make good our paffage over it.

We paffed many villages, and were now travelling through a country like a continued garden, abounding in trees and plants of various kinds. At four in the afternoon we came to a kind of arcade, within which was a charming fountain of water; but the Bedouins, feized with the panic of their camels, ftopped fhort, and refufed to enter, until one of their number had reconnoitred the place. Paffing feveral water-mills, and a burying-ground, we at laft perceived, at a fmall diftance before us, the walls of a great town. The numbers of dead indicated by the multitude of grave-ftones, the rich appearance of the adjacent country, and many fine

fine gardens along the road, fuggefted the idea of a very extenfive city. After proceeding a confiderable way on the outfide of the town-wall, we were about to halt for refrefhment, when we received a meffage from the bafha, ordering us inftantly to depart, and at the fame time threatening us with the whole weight of his difpleafure in cafe of difobedience. Senfible that we were at the mercy of a tyrant, we thought it expedient to withdraw to fome diftance; but foon received a fimilar notice, and I began to imagine that the terror of the inhabitants, at the approach of armed Bedouins, is fo great that every one trembles for his own fecurity, while they remain in his neighbourhood. Meanwhile a bold Arab, highly incenfed at the infolence of the people, and whofe patience was unable to brook any further interruption, ftooped his dromedary, and ftuck his lance in the ground, to denote his right of poffeffion; and, in fpite of the reproaches and abufe poured upon us from the furrounding gardens, the whole band inftantly followed his example. On the third of Auguft, therefore,

fore, and on the thirty-fifth day since our departure from Baffora, we fixed our quarters in the vicinity of this city.

Our marches and counter-marches in the desert had occasioned in me such a confusion of ideas, respecting the direction of our route, that I now found it extremely difficult to determine by my maps the place of our present encampment. Having observed that the general line of our march was greatly to the W. of Aleppo, I could find nothing in my geographical computations, at our supposed distance from the sea, that could at all correspond to it, but the ancient city of Damascus. I asked my companions if this was not the name of the town; but was answered, that it was called *Chams,* or the City of the Sun; that it was governed by a very powerful basha; and that the name of my country had never yet reached the ears of the inhabitants. It was added, that the people were a peculiarly vicious and malevolent race; and indeed I was not misinformed, if I may depend, as a proof, on those horrid curses and execrations regularly poured out against the Turks,

Turks, as often as the Bedouins returned from market. Respecting our actual situation on the globe, however, I was now more in the dark than before; and, being told that Aleppo was still at the distance of ten days journey, I urged my conductor to set out with me soon for that place. In the mean time I was faint with hunger and fatigue, and therefore sent immediately to Chams for provisions, which we devoured with great eagerness the moment they were set before us. I bathed to refresh my weary limbs, changed my dress, and made it my business to profit by the present interval of repose.

I now entreated my conductor to lead me to some inn or house of entertainment for strangers; but, to a man whose notions and habits of life were so little familiar to European manners, my proposal appeared idle and ridiculous. Besides, he was under no small concern, lest I should be molested, and even insulted by the Turks. Next day, having expressed my desire of making some acquaintance with the Asiatic Christians, he with great readiness introduced me to a

man

man of the Syriac ritual, from whom I learned, that Chams is the name the Arabs give to Damafcus. I met afterwards with a father Jefuit in the ftreets, dreffed in the fafhion of the country, who, upon hearing I was a native of France, affured me he was of the fame nation, and invited me to an afylum in his *hofpice* or convent; a favour which I accepted with much pleafure and alacrity.

The city of Damafcus is large and populous. The houfes, in front of the ftreets, are very indifferent; but prefent a handfome appearance towards the gardens. It contains manufactures of various kinds; and the market-places are well conftructed, and ornamented with a rich colonade of variegated marble. The ftreets, in general, are tolerably broad; but the diftrict frequented by the Chriftians is mean, and in all refpects much inferior to the other quarters of the town.

The great trade and population of Damafcus, as well as the high veneration in which it is held by Muffulmen, are owing to its being the place of general rendez-
vous

vous for the Mahometan pilgrims of Europe, and the northern parts of Syria, on their way to Mecca, a circumstance which has bestowed on it the title of Mahomet's Heel.

The caravan of Mecca is conducted by the basha of Damascus, who receives a considerable sum from the Porte on this account, as well as to maintain a military force, and to keep certain castles on the desert in repair. These forts are to defend the pilgrim wells against the ravages of the Arabs, who are regularly paid a certain tribute by the caravan, for liberty to pass unmolested. They are joined, at a certain distance from Damascus, by the caravans of Bagdad and Grand Cairo; in the first of which are pilgrims from all the southern parts of Asia, and in the latter similar followers of their prophet from the different tribes and nations of Africa. As the caravan's arrival at Mecca is fixed for the two great solemnities, the feast of Courban Beyran, or Abraham's sacrifice, and that of Beyran, or the Turkish carnival, at the end of Ramadan, and corresponding to the Jewish

ish passover, it must not be detained at Damascus beyond the fixed period of its departure, under any pretext whatever.

The Jesuits of Damascus shewed me every attention and civility in their power; and indeed the hospitality they afforded me in a city which, properly speaking, does not contain one resident European, and where the manners of the people are uncommonly cruel and ferocious, was the most grateful and seasonable of all the instances of kindness I received in the whole course of my travels. These good fathers, lastly, found me a guide to *Baruth*, on the borders of the Mediterranean, four days journey from Damascus. After passing nearly a week in their *hospice*, I bade adieu to my friends the Jesuits.

CHAP. XVIII.

The Author quits Damafcus, and paffes through a mountainous but fertile country.—Hofpitality and excellent character of the mountaineers.—Arrival at Baruth, and departure thence for Quefrouan.—The Author vifits feveral convents, and arrives at the hofpice of Aintoura.

HAVING fet out from Damafcus for Baruth, with the mountains, as formerly, on the right, a tolerable road led us to their fummit; and at ten o'clock, after eight hours march, we put up at a fmall village. Though the foil is extremely dry, with little appearance of cultivation, I found here excellent fruit, milk, and vegetables. Refuming our journey in the courfe of the night, after afcending and defcending for a confiderable time, we entered a narrow defile of great length, which brought us to a large and extenfive plain named Beca, fomewhat marfhy, but with

a black

a black and fertile foil. Near to the centre of this plain we croffed a fmall river, and foon came to a village, which ferves as a depofit for moft of the grain raifed in the neighbouring parts of the country. We left this village at our ufual hour of the night, and afcended high and craggy mountains, which, however, were cultivated as much as appeared compatible with the nature and quantity of the foil: the difficulty and fatigue of afcending and defcending thefe mountains were fo great, that feveral of our mules fell lame, and we were obliged to continue our progrefs on foot.

As every inch of the little foil the natives owe to nature is planted with vineyards, mulberry, and other fruit-trees, we were well fupplied upon the road with fruits of various kinds, which grow in abundance amongft thefe wild and difmal rocks. We ftopped to take fome refrefhment at a cottage, where I obferved the remains of a confiderable fountain, which formerly ufed to water the mulberry-trees in its vicinity.

The Afiatic method of cultivating the mulberry-tree is different from that in ufe among

among Europeans. According to the latter, though at a certain feafon the tree is deprived of its leaves, ftill it is permitted to rife to its full growth; whereas, by the former, at the fame time it is ftripped of its leaves it is lopped of its branches; hence the mulberry-tree of eaftern countries is feldom above eight or nine feet high.

In this country I was every where hofpitably received. The common food of the inhabitants confifts of fweet and four milk, and a fort of crape-cakes toafted on a cylinder of hewn ftone, which is heated withinfide. The milk of this country I found much better than that of the defert, which was not only four, but hardened to the confiftency of a flint ftone.

The natives of the mountains have a noble fimplicity of character, equally removed from the domineering arrogance of the Turk, and that mean fervility of fpirit, which, I am forry to fay, feems to debafe the Chriftian vifage within the walls of Damafcus. The Chriftians of that city, partly owing to Mahometan tyranny, and partly to their own daftardly behaviour, are

VOL. II. M fubjected

subjected to the condition, and merit the appellation, of slaves, rather than the character of men.

We proceeded on our journey during the night, though at the short distance of five or six leagues from Baruth; and having arrived at the top of the mountains, at length came in view of the Mediterranean, when I gave thanks to the Almighty for having conducted me to the prospect of that sea which washes the shores of my native country. The sky was overcast, and we had the first shower of rain. I had met with in these climates, while the regions of the atmosphere, fraught with vast masses of vapour, towering with magnificence in various forms and elevations, presented an appearance which was far from being familiar to my late observation. On the frigid summits of these mountains, however, I could not help feeling some regret for the warmer climates I was leaving behind me.

In our gradual descent from the heights we came in view of an extensive plain, whose lively verdure was singularly grateful to the eye. As we proceeded, the springs, pouring

pouring down from the ridges, gently watered or entirely overflov ed the fkirts of the mountains; and hence the charming verdure of thofe little patches of good ground which are found interfperfed among the rocks. The rivulets, uniting their ftreams in their progrefs towards the bottom of the mountain, formed little noify torrents, which again diverging into various channels, after wafhing the roots of the hills, moiftened and fertilized the adjacent plain. We arrived at a little fort or caftle, fituated on a fmall river, which being above the level of a great plantation of mulberries, watered them with all the advantage of the moft feafonable and fertilizing fhowers. Through thefe plantations we profecuted our journey, and met with a foil fo highly cultivated, that it was difficult to difcover a fingle foot of wafte or fallow ground; water, however, becomes more fcarce, in proportion as the traveller refnoves from the foot of the mountains. We now came in view of Baruth, where we arrived with eafe at nine in the morning. I alighted at the cuftomhoufe, whence, after feeing my things examined,

M 2

mined, I went to a convent of Capuchin friars, where the good fathers gave me a kind and hofpitable reception.

I had a letter from the jefuits of Damafcus to the fuperior of a convent of that order in the Quefrouan, a diftrict of Lebanon inhabited only by the Maronites, whom I was defirous to vifit. I received all the information I wanted from the fuperior of this convent, whofe placid but animated countenance was an index of the delicacy and fenfibility of his mind, as well as of that pure and unaffected zeal by which he was actuated in the functions of his miffion. I paffed only two days in this town, which is inconfiderable in fize, and miferably built. Baruth, as well as a great part of the neighbouring mountains, is under the jurifdiction of an emir, who is tributary to the Turks; a circumftance to which the people owe their fecurity from Ottoman oppreffion. In this city Chriftians and Mahometans live on friendly terms, partly owing to the rigour of public juftice, which is adminiftered with great impartiality, and partly to that prompt vengeance which is generally

rally inflicted on the fpot by the party aggrieved.

I now departed for Quefrouan, after hearing it much extolled for its natural ftrength, an advantage arifing from thofe lofty mountains with which it is furrounded, as well as from the population and native valour of the people. I had likewife heard that I fhould find there many convents of both fexes; that the rites of the Romifh religion were as freely exercifed in Quefrouan as in any province of France; and, in a word, that thefe mountaineers granted toleration to no other religious fect whatever.

With thefe and fimilar impreffions on my mind, I paffed a little river in the plains of Baruth, and continuing my journey by the fea fhore on the road to Tripoli, I came to the foot of a mountain, which is only to be afcended by flights of fteps cut in the folid rock. This is one of thofe great works which continue to preferve the memory of the Romans, many of whofe infcriptions on this road ftill meet the eye of the traveller. All along the path, which is about twelve feet broad, they had ufed used the precaution to chissel holes corresponding to the hoofs of their horses, in order to prevent them from slipping or falling on the stones. Rails have been very properly placed on the side next to the sea, which heaves its billows with great violence, and to a great height, against the rocks, whilst towards land the head of the traveller becomes giddy as he looks down upon the frightful precipice.

Having ascended this extraordinary tract, which is by no means difficult, and descended in the same manner on the opposite side, I passed what is called Dog's River, at two leagues distance from Baruth. Towards the sea I observed a plantation of mulberry-trees, which received necessary supplies of moisture from that river, by means of various canals. I now struck off to the right, and ascending the banks of the river, which at first are much confined by steep rocks, but afterwards open into a little valley planted with mulberry-trees, I came on the left to a mountain, gradually rising into the form of an amphitheatre, and planted with different kinds of timber. I forded

I forded Dog's river above a confiderable bridge, on which I found an infcription, and afcending by a path extremely fteep and difficult, I at laft reached the top of the mountain, and paid my refpects to a Maronite convent named Louifey, whofe church is tolerably neat and clean. I difcovered from thence on a hill the Jefuits hofpice of Aintoura, to which I was directed, and in my way towards it paffed a populous village. I croffed a narrow valley, which, though the foil is watered with few fprings, and confequently lefs fertile than the lower grounds, is covered, like all others in this country, with fig-trees, mulberry-trees, and vineyards. Purfuing a gradual afcent along the fide of the mountain, I left a little to the right a large village ftanding on a fine champain country in good cultivation, and after travelling about a league further on the fame ridge, I obferved on a little eminence before me a convent of nuns, who are under the infpection of the Jefuits; and at length arrived at the hofpice of Aintoura, fituated two leagues from the river of Dogs.

CHAP.

CHAP. XIX.

Description of the hospice of Aintoura, and the mountain on which it is situated.—The author proceeds to Jelton, and visits the Cheik or lord of the country.—His stay at the house of this Cheik, and the visits he pays to several others.—Description of the village of Jelton.—Police, customs, and religious rites of the inhabitants of the province of Quesrouan.

I WAS well received by the superior, delivered him a letter from Damascus, and, expressing an earnest desire to visit Quesrouan, he engaged to afford me every means in his power of gratifying my wishes. This religious house is situated at a third of the whole height to the top of a mountain, which, though extremely steep and difficult of ascent, is cultivated and planted to the very summit; the soil is particularly dry and stony, and yet the trees and vines appear fresh and in every respect in good condition,

condition. The houfes are not collected in the manner of villages, but thinly fcattered all over the mountain. Befides the convent of nuns above mentioned, there is higher on the mountain a feminary, in which the jefuits educate a number of young men deftined to the fervice of the altar. The ftudents were at this time greatly incumbered by a princefs, widow of a certain emir, who, upon her embracing the Romifh religion, had requefted permiffion to refide for fome time in the feminary.

By means of the fuperior I became acquainted with a cheik or lord of the country, who lives at two leagues diftance, in a village named Jelton. The greateft part of the Chriftian cheiks related to the reigning family, which is very numerous, and divided into different branches, refide in this village. On the third day of my vifit to the Quefrouan jefuits, the fuperior gave me a letter to this cheik, and I refumed my journey.

Having afcended to a confiderable height, I paffed a fmall wood of pines, and looked down on the vallies of Aintoura on one hand,

hand, and to a vaſt plain bounded by the river of Dogs, and the amphitheatrical mountains of the Antiquefrouan, on the other: I ſaw the eſtate of the emir Solyma, but the village in which he reſides was covered from my view by the interpoſition of a ſmall hill.

On the confines of the plain above mentioned are the ſources of the river of Dogs, which is augmented by the junction of other rivers, in their deſcent from the top of the valley. Theſe ſources take their riſe in two very deep caverns; the firſt, formed in the rock, is of great capacity, and preſents to the eye a multitude of beautiful cryſtallizations ſuſpended from the roof: the ſecond, which is lower and more difficult of acceſs, beſides many other cryſtals with which it is adorned, detaches one from the vault in the form of a pillar, and about the thickneſs of a man's body, to the diſtance of a foot from the ground. The traveller may obſerve, through a hole in the rock, the river riſing from its ſource, which ruſhing in a body under thoſe vaſt caverns, produces a tremendous noiſe. I aſcended a very

very high mountain, at the bottom of which is the refidence of a bifhop, and near its fummit the village of Jelton. Notwithftanding the foil continues dry and ftony, the mulberry-trees thrive in a furprifing manner. This village makes a better appearance than thofe I had hitherto feen; though the houfes announce any thing rather than the manfions of cheiks, or the great nobility of the country: their inhabitants, however, united in intereft and affection, are contented to maintain a very frugal but independent manner of life. Their perfons fuggeft the idea of an opulent peafantry, much more than that of a race of mighty chiefs; but from this extreme fimplicity of manners, and inexperience of luxury, refult that courage and magnanimity by which thefe mountaineers perfevere in afferting their freedom and almoft entire independence of the Turkifh government. They pay to the Porte a fmall annual tribute with great punctuality; nor have they ever been tempted, by the natural ftrength and advantages of their fituation, to feek a complete exemption from the Ottoman yoke.

I alighted

I alighted at the houfe of the cheik, to whom I had a letter from the fuperior of Aintoura; he was abroad, but I faw fome of his family amufing themfelves under an arbour. They invited me with much civility to join them; and it was not long before I had a very hofpitable reception from the cheik himfelf. He recommended me to the care of his fon, charging him not to lofe fight of me, and to fhew me whatever was moft interefting in the country, and beft calculated to gratify my curiofity. He obliged me to pafs three days at his houfe, after which I went to vifit feveral others of this highland nobility, in whofe houfes I was regularly ferved with a collation fimilar to what had been fet before me in the female convent, and in the families of fome refugee merchants at Aintoura. I affifted at all their affemblies, which are ufually held under the fhade of trees; and was conducted in the fame eafy manner to divine fervice, and an evening party, confifting of the youth of both fexes from the neighbourhood. In this affembly, after allotting a confiderable portion of time to

the

the amufement of converfation, one of the company reads part of a book on fome religious fubject, and the evening concludes with the recital of prayers. I was furprized to find among the inhabitants of thefe mountains fo much civility, and even urbanity of manners; the cheik's fon, in particular, who was my friend and conductor in all my excurfions, difcovered a fweetnefs of temper and difpofition uncommonly interefting.

This village is fituated on a dry and ftony foil, and has the advantage of no other water than what is contained in deep wells and cifterns; but its impregnable ftrength, arifing from its lofty fituation on the third gradation of this mountainous amphitheatre, was no doubt the great inducement which engaged the lords of Quefrouan to make choice of it for their ufual refidence.

In the cheiks is vefted the landed property of the whole country, from which they derive a certain revenue; charged, however, with a fixed fum to the emir, who, in his turn, pays a fmall annual tribute

bute to the Porte. They administer justice within the bounds of their own estates, and assess the people in their proportion of the public burthens. In all other respects the distinctions of rank are better understood in Europe than among the mountains of Quesrouan, where every man is at liberty to know and feel his own value and consequence. The Catholics are alone regarded as the true and legitimate inhabitants of the country; and hence, on the road to Tripoli, which passes through its lower dependencies, the Turks are subjected to a certain toll, from which all Christians are exempted.

The people are never seen at any distance from their villages without being completely armed; and among them no personal insult is ever suffered to pass with impunity. The aspect of the natives has an expression of confidence widely differing from an air of impudence or effrontery, and conveying an idea of goodness and affability, united to great intrepidity of mind. They are prone to compassion and the offices of hospitality;

are

are gay and lively in their ordinary deportment; and difcover on fome occafions a confiderable talent for irony.

The clergy in this country are poor, and labour with their own hands to fupport their families; for though Catholics, being of a ritual different from the Latin, a man may take orders fubfequent to marriage, provided it has been contracted with a virgin. Here, therefore, a prieft feldom remains long in a ftate of celibacy; and his conduct in this refpect is extremely agreeable to the tafte of his people. Divine fervice is celebrated in the Syriac language, but the gofpels and breviary are read aloud in the Arabic, which is the vulgar tongue in all countries bordering on Arabia. As the ftudies of the clergy are almoft entirely confined to the fcriptures and the catechifm of the church, they are very little converfant in abftrufe queftions of theology; but they are regular in their lives, found in their morals, and fincere in what they believe. Speculative tenets might create a fpirit of controverfy, engender new opinions, and have a dangerous tendency to fhake

their

their prefent implicit fubmiffion and obedience to the fee of Rome.

Our miffionaries are extremely ufeful here, and in other parts of Syria, not only by inftructing the true Catholics, but in converting fuch to the Latin ritual as have been enfnared into the erroneous opinions of fchifm or herefy. The Catholic faith has made confiderable progrefs at Damafcus, as well as in the parts S. W. from the mountains, where the Syrians, Greeks, and Arminians, ufed to be few, compared with the fchifmatics and heretics of different denominations. The religion of Rome has alfo, by the fame means, penetrated into Egypt, where I am informed a number of Cophti have fubmitted to the doctrines and authority of the church. Some of them, however, in deference to the manners and cuftoms of their country, admit of circumcifion in both fexes, a practice in direct oppofition to a decree exprefsly paffed againft it in the court of Rome.

It is to be hoped that the pious induftry of thefe men may ftill extend the fphere of its operation, particularly on the fide of Abyffinia,

Abyssinia, where, considering the frequency, simplicity, and honesty of Christian heretics, there is every reason to believe that the truly apostolic missionary might reap a considerable harvest. I had occasion to observe the unwearied pains taken by this description of men, in Turkey, Persia, and the nations of India, all abounding in Christians ill instructed, and without the means of better information—how sincerely is it to be regretted that their number is so very small! Considering the many discouragements the missionary meets with in the East, from regulations of national police, one cannot sufficiently admire his success in the kingdoms of Pegu, Siam, Cambodia, Cochinchina, and China. A few natives of China, who were educated some time since in an Italian seminary, have rendered eminent services to their countrymen in matters of religion.

The answer made by the king of Spain, to one who urged the impolicy of retaining possession of the Philippine isles, from the heavy expence with which they burthened the public, deserves to be recorded:

corded: He defired, he faid, no other produce from thefe iflands than the fruits of his miffion; and he would be fatisfied if, among the millions of Chriftian profelytes, added to the church fince their firft fubmiffion to the crown of Spain, there were one poor Indian, whofe name fhould be found at laft written in the book of life. It may be juftly faid of Spain, that fhe has made more Chriftians in Afia and America than fhe has fubjects in the whole extent of her European dominions.—But I return to Quefrouan.

The impregnable fituation of this country having naturally pointed it out as an afylum for all the profeffors of Chriftianity in Afiatic Turkey, it has become the refidence of many bifhops, and the feat of a confiderable number of convents for both fexes. Among the former are the patriarch of the Greek church; the patriarch of Antioch, who prefides over the fect of the Maronites; and the patriarch of Armenia, who fuperintends feveral convents under the rules of his own ritual. The people in general are fond of religion; and though

vice

vice and immorality find their way into all countries, they are, however, much lefs prevalent in the mountains than in the plain. The women do not live under the fame rigorous difcipline, nor are they fecluded from public view nearly in the fame degree as in the towns; but if an unmarried woman has the misfortune to become pregnant, fhe expiates with her life, and by the hands of her own relations, the folly and weaknefs of her conduct. A mother who has given her daughter in marriage, would confider herfelf and family greatly difhonoured, if after confummation her fon-in-law fhould not produce proofs of the virtue of his bride. A like cuftom prevails among the natives of Mexico.

CHAP. XX.

The Author quits Jelton, and makes excursions among the high mountains.—He arrives at the village of Mafra, and is hospitably received by a priest.— Rural mode of life of the inhabitants.

I LEFT Jelton on the third day after my arrival; and, conceiving that the most elevated ridges, being little frequented by strangers, must present the manners of the people in their true and genuine colours, I took the route towards Mafra, a village situated at the foot of the highest mountain in the province of Quefrouan, and where the natives feed their flocks in the summer season. After an hour's walk I ascended to a convent amidst dismal and arid rocks, whence, however, issues a plentiful spring of water, which diffuses moisture and a charming verdure over all the soil in their vicinity. The vivid green of these

these earthy patches, and the brown parched furface of the rocks, which briftle like needles in the air all around, form a ftriking contraft to the eye. In the monaftery, however, fituated in the centre of this horrid fcene, a right reverend prelate has chofen to take up his abode.

I afcended confiderably higher, and, arriving at the village of *Claat,* where the foil is fertile, lefs ftony, and covered with trees in a frefh and thriving ftate, I refted fome time, in company with a cheik of humane and obliging manners. Having refumed my journey, after walking half an hour I came to the confines of a valley, where I looked down a precipice to a narrow glen, fcarcely affording room for a large torrent, which rolled its waters with great noife and impetuofity over immenfe fragments of rocks. I defcended, and having croffed the torrent at a bridge clofe to a water-mill, I began to climb a mountain on the oppofite fide, which I found particularly difficult. I was a good deal fatigued before I reached the top; but my perfeverance at length brought me to the profpect of a beautiful country, planted with the fineft mulberry-trees I had yet feen. Springs in abundance diftil from the heights upon a fertile foil, without a ftone, and prefenting over the wide extent of this natural amphitheatre a neat and level furface. Beneath the mulberry-trees the ground produces roots and vegetables of different kinds. I at laft arrived at the village of Maira, fituated on the declivity of a high hill, which appeared every where ftudded with houfes, at the diftance of three leagues and a half from Jelton. I was much pleafed with the beauty of the fcene, and little repined at the toil I had experienced in climbing up to my prefent elevated fituation.

The cheik at Jelton having given me a letter to the minifter of the parifh, I alighted at his door. He was not at home, but I was admitted to his wife and feveral of his children. The good woman received me in the beft manner, and preffed me to wait her hufband's return, and to repofe myfelf after my fatigue. I obferved, with the moft pleafant emotions, the wife of the

fimple

simple pastor of Mafra, who was at this moment working in his field, and who I had no doubt would enter his porch in an equally rustic appearance with that of his spouse. She was a fine woman, in the bloom of youth, considerably advanced in pregnancy, and with a complexion deeply bronzed by the sun. In the midst of three children, whom she endeavoured to quiet by turns, she conducted the detail of her little family affairs. How much I admired this precious and simple manner of living! In a kind of open gallery, which served for a parlour, she spread a little bed on the ground, in order to lay her infant to sleep; casting her eye occasionally to a stove, where she boiled some slices of gourd in a kettle. She dressed some eggs and milk in separate dishes, with crape-cakes, for my supper. At one time she seemed to assure me by her looks of all the inclination in the world to entertain me well; at another she could not conceal her impatience for her husband. Meanwhile the good man arrived from his farm; and his attentions to his guest seemed to vie with the kind civilities he had juft received from his wife. In compliance, however, with the reftraints which Oriental manners impofe on the behaviour of women, fhe foon withdrew, and gave up all her attention to the concerns of her family. At the hour for evening *vefpers*, the people affembled in the open air, where prayers were recited as much in the fpirit of true piety, and confequently in a manner equally acceptable in the eye of the Deity, as if we had been feated under the gilded ceiling of the moft fumptuous temple. His flock feemed defirous of my company, and were at pains to difcover by what means they might amufe me moft agreeably.

The evening brought home a number of domeftic animals in flocks, which conftituted the whole wealth of this honeft ecclefiaftic. Affifted by his wife he fed them by hand, and received their careffes, the only return they could make for the care and kindnefs of their mafter; a fituation, however, extremely interefting, and which tends to illuftrate thofe gentle

and

and innocent manners so prevalent among the Asiatics.

At my own desire, my bed was laid in a raised corner under the porch, and my host reposed close by me and my conductor; for, according to the manners of the mountaineers, the master of a family is himself the keeper and guardian of his guests; a rule of hospitality which was religiously observed respecting me by the cheik's son at Jelton. Besides, as the customs of the East do not permit strangers to sleep under the same roof with the women, visitors are always lodged under the porch, or in the apartments named Mansoul, which have no communication whatever with the principal part of the house. I slept extremely well; but, owing to the cold and keen air of these lofty mountains, which are a continuation of the famous Mount Lebanon, I caught a slight rheumatism, which, however, the genial warmth of the next day entirely removed.

As soon as it was day, I attended my host to the celebration of mass; after which, notwithstanding the most pressing invitation

invitation to prolong my vifit, I refumed my journey, and proceeded towards what is efteemed the higheft mountain in the country. On account of the climate there is no human habitation higher than the village of Mafra, which is itfelf covered with fnow during fix months of the year.

We paffed the fkirts of fome mulberry plantations belonging to Mafra, where the foil continues of equal fertility, and well watered, with few ftones. Upon afcending, however, a mountain of moderate height, the mulberry-trees entirely difappear, a circumftance probably owing to the foil's being feverely chilled by the continuance of the fnow. I now came to land in a ftate of nature, grazed by cattle of various kinds, which, a little farther on, the natives are ufed to fold during the night. I obferved fheep-folds, for the firft time, on the top of a little hill, whofe fides were fown with different kinds of grain. The fhepherds were employed in making cheefe of the milk they obtained in the morning; and here I ftopped to breakfaft, breakfaſt, in company with ſeveral inhabitants of Mafra.

CHAP. XXI.

Arrival at a fertile plain, on which ſeveral ancient ruins are diſcovered.—Deſcription of a temple of great antiquity, and other intereſting monuments.—The Author reaches the villages of Beſommar and Agoujta, where he is kindly received by the eccleſiaſtics.

I WAS now conducted a little higher to a rich and fertile plain, a ſhort league in length, and only a quarter in breadth, which was ſown in the ſame manner as the hill I have mentioned, and preſented a moſt pleaſing verdure to the eye. This extenſive field is bounded towards the ſouth by the great mountain, whoſe perpendicular rocks are loſt in the clouds; towards the eaſt and north by a ſmall hill; while

towards

towards the weft the eye flits over fucceffive chains of mountains to a great diftance. I furveyed the ruins of an ancient tower, in form nearly fquare, and built of huge ftones, fome of which, having their extremities fixed in oppofite walls, were of length fufficient to anfwer the purpofe of beams, while others were employed as lintils to the gates inftead of arches. Over the firft gate was an infcription in Greek characters, which it was not in my power to tranfcribe; but, in an angle of the building, on the outfide, I found another, of which I obtained a perfect copy, and which the Academy of Sciences at Paris have taken the trouble to tranflate: it marks the period at which the tower was erected, and not the age of the temple I am about to fpeak of, which is probably much more ancient, the mention of which it alfo makes.

ΓΕ ΝΤΕΠΙΤΘΛΜ ΡΛΒ ΒΟΜΟΥ ΕΠΜΕΛΗ-
ΤΟΥ ΕΚΤωΝΤΟΥ ΜΕΠΣΤΟΥ ΘΕΟΥ
ωΚΟΔΟ ΜΗΘΗ.
(doubtful)

" In

" In the three hundred and fifty-fifth
" year, Tholmus prefiding for the fixth
" time over the Temple of the Moft High
" God, this Building was erected."—The
period alluded to by this infcription is the
æra of the Seleucides, that is, three hundred and twelve years before the birth of
Jefus Chrift. Thefe ruins extend from the
tower weftward on the ample field already
defcribed, and conduct the traveller to others
of greater magnitude. The firft object
here that fixed my attention was a ftone,
which by its fize and fhape feemed to have
been employed as the bafe of an altar.
Befide it lay another, in the centre of whofe
plane appeared a raifed quadrangular fpace,
furrounded by a groove; this ftone, with
equal probability, might have ferved as
the table of an altar. I next obferved the
remains of a very wide gate, which externally had two galleries fronting each other.
At the end of each gallery was a large open
hall, adorned with pillars, whofe capitals,
ornamented with flowers and foliage in excellent fculpture, were ftrong indications of
the great extent and magnificence of this

very

very ancient building. Within the gate, and in the middle of a large area, my conductor shewed me a well of extraordinary depth. At the oppofite end of the temple was a gallery, which occupied the whole breadth of the building, and was fupported by a row of maffy pillars, fimilar to thofe already mentioned. Beyond this gallery were the ruins of a wall, and an area of a very large room, at the bottom of which lay other ruins, but I was unable to difcover what was under them, or whether they did not feparate us from another hall.

This very ancient and venerable temple is now almoft in ruins; the pillars, and a great proportion of the walls, lie fcattered in large fragments on the ground. Its fcite is amidft high perpendicular rocks, which in fome places ferved it for ramparts. According to the natives it was a temple, confecrated to the mother of the gods, under the reign of one of the Ptolemies, but which, they cannot pretend to fay; a tradition, however, which has probably been perverted in the circumftance in which it

differs

differs from the interpretation given of the infcription by the learned academy, efpecially as the only variety between them confifts in the word *mother* inftead of *father*, and thefe in the Arabic may be very eafily confounded. The diftrict in which thefe ruins are to be found is called, in the dialect of the country, Elfogra. It was in this quarter of Lebanon, if we may give credit to the tradition of the natives, where thofe ftately cedars grew, which were conveyed to Jerufalem, and ufed in the conftruction of Solomon's temple. However this may be, this auguft edifice, having the fame advantages of profpect with the adjacent plain, was erected in a moft delightful fituation.

From the ruins I accompanied my conductor to a rich fpring of fine limpid water, on the brink of which we fat down to dinner. Such is the very cold temperature of this water, that I was unable to hold my hand in it for any length of time. Several of the villagers of Mafra having favoured me with their company on this expedition, our provifions were a joint ftock, and after making an agreeable repaft we

§   continued

continued our progress to the right of the great mountain. The rocks contained Greek inscriptions; but as these consisted only of two or three letters, I did not take the trouble to transcribe them.

Ascending eastward, in the same direction, we came to other ruins, some of whose stones seemed perforated for the insertion of pipes, which might in former times have served for a fountain or jet-d'eau. These, therefore, were probably the ruins of a building, which had been erected as a *vista* to the temple, in the bottom of the plain.

Having reached the summit of the hill, we found ourselves on the Ass's Back, which slopes on one side into the plain, and on the other into a vale of great depth. Along this ridge runs a canal, which serves to conduct to Mafra the water I saw there in such plenty. I traced the canal for a quarter of a league, and came to a very steep mountain, where we found the copious source, whose bottom we could not perceive: from this reservoir two canals, each of which might contain three cubic feet, receive their ample supplies; but such is the intense cold of this water, that in drinking it one is in danger of lofing one's teeth; and I was apprehenfive it might affect my bowels. I have been fince told, what feems extremely probable, that thefe fprings are fed by the fnows of more northern mountains, which are melted by the fun, and afterwards filtrated through the rocks.

At the diftance of about two leagues from Mafra, the higher grounds being wholly uninhabited, I parted with my companions, who chofe to return to the village, and took a little refrefhment and repofe. They went back to Mafra; but though I meant to return to the fame place, I chofe to follow a different route, by the other branch of the canal, which flows from the above-mentioned fource.

My road foon led me to a natural arch, about forty paces broad, and four-fcore in length, than which I never faw a more majeftic fpecimen of nature's workmanfhip, or more nearly approaching in many refpects to the execution of art. The water, pouring from the heights during the melting of the snow, gradually unites in a great torrent, which, precipitating itself, forms a cascade about forty feet high, pursues its course with increased rapidity amongst rifted rocks, and at length passes under this arch, fifty paces perhaps below the fall. The vault of the arch, though on a level with the road, is at least one hundred feet above the bed of the torrent, which here begins to enter the mouth of a little valley. The opposite banks serve as abutments to the extremities of the arch, which has all the neatness of effect that could have been expected from the skill and dexterity of an architect. It is difficult to say by what means nature, after having penetrated the solid mass of steep rocks, contrived to smooth and polish it into the form of a fine arch, with all the regularity and precision of the chizzel. Probably the violence of the current first made an impression on the less compact parts at its base, where having at length pierced and undermined the huge block, it afterwards gradually filed it away in this uniform manner, from an equal degree of refiftance being every where oppofed to the force of the torrent.

Paffing this curious arch, and making a fweep round the fide of the mountain, I entered fome pleafant and fertile fields. In a recefs of the mountain I faw the fources of the river *la Croix*, which I had paffed in my way to Mafra. Keeping ftill on the fkirts of the mountain, I paffed various beautiful cafcades, and came to a large valley well watered, and producing a kind of fmall grain. La Croix, befides fupplying a canal cut along the declivity of the oppofite mountain, furnifhes water to two others of a larger fize. Croffing this valley I afcended a high earthy hill, where the foil became more fandy, and lefs fertile, than in the preceding parts of my excurfion. Turning off to the right, I arrived at a handfome village, whence we had a view of Mafra, fituated on a neighbouring eminence. This hamlet is in the vicinity of a place named *Haragges*, and furrounded with fine mulberry-trees excellently fupplied with water. I paffed fome poor ftony ground, little fufceptible of cultivation; and left on my right a number of small vallies, apparently of great fertility. I now arrived on the borders of a little plain, on which stand a church and convent containing only one monk and a friar, detached in the manner of a little colony from a more populous monastery: here we passed the night, and had no reason to complain of our entertainment. Next day after mass, having breakfasted, for in this country it is against every rule of hospitality to suffer a stranger to depart without eating, we resumed our journey, and passed over a miserable soil, covered sometimes with sand, and sometimes with large stones, similar to what we had seen the preceding evening. The produce of this district was chiefly pines, and herds of goats. At nine o'clock we saw a handsome church, at a village called Besommar, which is the residence of the Armenian patriarch. After paying respects to his eminence, I took some refreshment, and continued my journey. I descended lower on the mountain, and then turned to the right, entering upon a strong soil,

in

in all refpects like that of Aintoura and Jelton. Defcending to a fecond ridge, which commands a profpect of the fea, I faw the village of Agoufta below, and on our right at fome diftance that of Gazar. In the firft, befides feveral cheiks, refides the venerable patriarch of the fect of the Maronites of Antioch, at whofe manfion I ftopped, and was received with much politenefs and affection. I had the honour to dine with this good man, who in the courfe of our converfation fpoke Latin and Italian with great correctnefs and fluency. One of his grand vicars favoured me with his conftant attendance; and about four o'clock, when the patriarch awaked from his nap, I took an affectionate leave. We walked round the village, which is moft agreeably fituated on the declivity of a very high mountain, cultivated in the form of a wild amphitheatre, and interfperfed with gardens and mulberry plantations. The houfes are fcattered all over an area in the form of a horfe-fhoe, with its opening towards the fea, for fuch is the appearance of the mountain, and extend down to the bottom, where the ground rifes into another ridge, which is well watered, and ſtill very high above the plain. The whole of this mountain is well cultivated; and in the middle of the village, oppofite to the houfe of a cheik, is a copious fpring of excellent water. The fituation of the village is extremely beautiful; but fometimes about noon, clouds, attracted by the lofty tops of the mountains, produce an obfcurity, and a thick mift, which I apprehend to be infalubrious.

CHAP.

CHAP. XXII.

The Author concludes his romantic excursion, and returns to Baruth.—He repairs from thence to Sidon, with a view to obtain a passage to France, but is disappointed.— He makes a considerable stay at Sidon, at the house of the French consul.—The antiquities in Sidon and its environs described.— Habits and sentiments of the natives of the mountains.

QUITTING this village, I crossed the mountain, passed a stony barren region, and came in view of the hospice of Arissa, which belongs to the fathers of the Holy Land, or the Recollects of St. Francis. After an hour's walk from Agousta, I arrived at this religious mansion. The hospice or convent is situated on the summit of a mountain, at a little distance from the sea, of which it commands an extensive prospect; but standing

upon

upon a poor foil, and having no water, except what is preferved in cifterns, it is upon the whole a barren and dreary retreat. I departed next day early, and after defcending towards the inland country, and travelling in the fkirts of the mountains, which are extremely painful and difficult, I at length reached a narrow dale watered by a beautiful rivulet. I afcended on the other fide, and fkirted the mountains, and foon came in fight of Aintoura, fituated on an adjacent hill. The intervening ground is very uneven, but not fo wild and rugged as the high mountain I had juft traverfed. I arrived at Aintoura on the fixth day; and having, after dinner, thanked the fuperior for all his kind offices, I began to defcend towards the plain.

I reached Baruth in the evening, after an abfence of ten days, which had been fpent in exploring the mountains of Quefrouan. The prior of the Capuchin convent received me with his ufual civility; from him I learned that a king's chebec had arrived from France on a cruize
off

off the coaft of Syria. Having obtained further information that this veffel, then at the ifland of Cyprus, was expected in a few days to enter the port of Sidon; and as that city was only diftant eight leagues, I propofed inftantly to fet out, in hopes of meeting fome old companions, with whom I had ferved at Toulon. Accordingly, on the 25th of Auguft, I proceeded to Sidon, and waited upon the French conful, who fhewed me much kindnefs, and offered to accommodate me with quarters in his houfe. He confirmed the prior's information refpecting the arrival of a French chebec; but I learned fome days after, that fhe had quitted Cyprus, and had failed for Candia, in order to join other fhips of the fame fquadron. Difappointed in my views, I refolved to proceed directly to Acre, perfuaded that the frequent arrivals there from the port of Marfeilles muft render my paffage to France much lefs precarious.

My fame as a traveller feemed to have made fome impreffion on the mind of
the

the conful, for he made many enquiries concerning my late expedition, and preſſed me to ſpend a little time longer in his family; urging, as reaſons for my compliance, the extreme fatigue I had ſuffered in the deſert, and the deranged ſtate of my health. He obſerved that the remains of an eruption on my ſkin, which had made its appearance in the country of the Marattas, proved that my blood was greatly heated; and as I was deſirous to ſtudy the character of the mountaineers, I ought to conſider them more extenſively, and avoid forming a haſty opinion from a curſory view, or rather from the appearance of a few individuals. Although a long ſecluſion from the company of women had produced in me a ruſticity of manners as well as appearance, his wife ſeemed to be of the ſame mind with her huſband, and united in entreaties that I would remain their gueſt for ſome time longer. The reſolution I had taken, to ſail directly for France, began to be ſhaken. The weak ſtate of my health, an eruption on my ſkin, and above all, the additional pleaſure

fure I had in profpect among thefe mountains, feemed on this occafion to fufpend the ordinary vigour of my mind; and the frefh knowledge, fo agreeable to my tafte, which I hoped to acquire in my intercourfe with the neighbouring Arabs, apologized for what, however, I could not help tacitly regarding as arifing from a facility of temper. About a month after my arrival I was feized with a regular fever; but the ufe of emetics, and the great care and attention of the conful and his family, gradually reftored me to health.

In the environs of Sidon the eye is delighted with the delicious verdure of many fine profpects. The rich gardens and orchards, which are excellently watered, diffufe over the face of the country the appearance of one continued foreft, confifting of various fruit-trees, together with the vine, which is permitted to grow here in all its luxuriance.

In the mountains of the neighbourhood are many caverns excavated in the rocks, with ten or twelve cells in each, according to their fize. Thefe, according to tradition, are

are the tombs of the ancient inhabitants of
Sidon ; but I am rather inclined to believe
they were places of retreat for the natives of the mountains. A caftle is fhewn
built by St. Louis ;—fome pillars of marble
and floors of jafper in Mofaic, are the
principal remains of antiquity that now
exift of this once beautiful and flourifhing
city.

On the ifland of Java are feveral mofques,
fcarce meriting the attention of the curious;
but in the vicinity of this town I obtained
accefs to a very confiderable one. This
building is of a quadrangular form, and is
erected, like all other mofques, according
to the direction of its fcite relatively to
Mecca. The firft object I remarked was a
rail at the bottom of the mofque, within
which was a model of Abraham's houfe at
Mahomet's grave. Rows of lamps, ornamented with oftrich's eggs, appeared fuf-
pended from the ceiling, at the diftance of
feven or eight feet from the ground. The
floor was covered with a clean handfome mat
for the proftrations of believers ; a religious
ceremony which they conftantly perform
with

with the face towards Mecca. This mode of adoration confifts in quick and frequent proftrations, and does not in all probability owe its origin to Mahomet, fince in the Chriftian worfhip of thefe parts we find a fimilar practice: it is, however, an expreffion of piety and devotion, of a nature noble and majeftic, and highly fuitable to thofe fentiments it is meant to exprefs.

Befides ftudying the rules and principles of the Arabic language, in which I was foon able to difcover much beauty, I was at pains to obtain every information in my power relative to the manners of the people who live among the adjacent mountains. That diftrict, which lies towards the S. W. is inhabited by a fect of Muffulmen, who are named *Mutuallis*, and are faid to have no connection with any other nation whatever. They obferve the fame diftance and referve towards ftrangers as the natives of India, neither inviting them to their houfes, nor eating with them from the fame difh; and though I cannot complain of having received the flighteft injury

injury during the time I paffed in their villages, I own, in their appearance, they have fomething peculiarly rude and ferocious. They tolerate Chriftians in the free exercife of their religion, who, happily, are much lefs the objects of their hatred and animofity than the Turks. Their dominion extends over the mountains all the way from Gebail to Balbec, including both towns, where they are reported to be much more favage in their manners than in the vicinity of Sidon. The mountains in the N. E. of Sidon are peopled by the Drufes, among whom Chriftianity enjoys an equal degree of toleration as among the Mutuallis.

The natives of thefe mountains are difaffected to the Turks, an antipathy partly owing to the influence of inveterate prejudice, and partly to a difference in matters of religious opinion. They are fenfible it is to their own bravery, and the inacceffible nature of their mountains, that they owe their happy independence. The Drufes are well affected towards Chriftians in general; but holding themfelves defcended ed from a French anceftry, who are faid to have taken refuge in thefe mountains at their expulfion from the Holy Land, at the end of the crufades, they have more than ordinary affection for the people of that country. The principles which, according to hiftorians, actuated the fubjects of the old man of the mountain, ftill influence the minds of fome individuals.

In the vicinity of Jerufalem I am told there is a race of Bedouin Arabs, who likewife affect to be defcended from the French. The Capuchin from whom I had this information had experienced many inftances of their partiality to his country, as had alfo a miffionary of the fame order, who refided among them for fome time in much credit and efteem.

CHAP.

CHAP. XXIII.

Obſervations on the fine climate and productions of the ſouthern parts of Syria.— Simple and induſtrious character of the inhabitants, contraſted with the luxury of Europe.—The monks of Syria deſcribed.— Reflections on celibacy and matrimony.

I WAS charmed with the beauty and ſerenity of this climate, which, in my opinion, is in a peculiar manner what a man who is deſirous of becoming the child of nature would wiſh to enjoy. In the different regions of the globe which I have viſited I have found no climate equally propitious to the natural ſtate of man with that which extends its mild influence over the ſouthern parts of Syria. In the countries ſituated between the tropics the rains fall almoſt inceſſantly during the ſix months of ſummer. The countries, on the contrary, a few degrees without the tropics, have but little rain,

rain, and that only in fpring and autumn, the feafons when it paffes from the cold to hotter regions of the earth. In Afia, on the confines of Baffora; in America, in the vicinity of Sartille; as well as in the defert regions of Africa, I have had occafion to remark that a fcarcity of rain, rendering the foil dry and inhofpitable, gradually reduces it to a dead fand. I will not pretend to affirm, however, that from this partial obfervation any rule can be drawn which fhall obtain univerfally; but the fact feems to be, that from the latitude of thirty to thirty-five degrees, the fix fummer months are entirely exempted from rain; whilft in the fucceeding period the cold is uniformly moderate, and one meets with many intervals of fine weather equal to the moft beautiful days in fummer.

In Syria a variety of grain fprings and comes to maturity during the winter months; a fact which affords undeniable evidence of what I have now been afferting. I acknowledge that there are certain fpecies of trees which then fhed their leaves; ftill, however, it is true, that in the month of November I have

have eaten new beans and peafe, while the gardens, abounding in flowers and vegetables, continue productive from that month till the opening of fummer. The particular fituation of Syria contributes a great deal to the excellency of its climate. It is protected from the north wind by an extenfive ridge of lofty mountains; it is bounded on the weft by the fea; and on the eaft by the arid deferts of Arabia, from whofe parched and fandy foil little vapour can arife to produce rain. Higher Egypt, and the country contiguous to Lima, are both finely fituated; but I believe the one and the other owe their dry and beautiful climates to fome high ridges, which intercept the progrefs of the clouds. In the neighbourhood of Lima the foil is fandy and barren, while Egypt owes her fertility to the induftry of her inhabitants, joined to the annual inundations of the Nile. The heat of fummer in higher Egypt is, befides, almoft intolerable; and every one knows that the Cophti as well as the Peruvian, groaning under the oppreffion of defpotifm, are highly taxed for the advantages of their climate.

Among

Among the productions of Syria are thofe of hot as well as cold climates; wheat, barley, cotton, the bamy or gombeau, the oak, the pine, and the fycamore, all grow in a great degree of perfection. The vine, the fig, the mulberry, the apple, and other trees of Europe, are no lefs common in the gardens and orchards, than the jujubier, the fig-bannan, the lemon, fweet and four, the orange, and the fugar-cane: all the roots and vegetable productions of thefe different climates are likewife found here in abundance.

The rites and ceremonies of the Catholic church are as regularly and openly performed in the bofom of the Syrian mountains, as in Paris or at Rome; with this difference, however, that as the manners of the people are more fimple, fo their devotion, as well as their morals, are proportionally purer in the former than in the latter.

The induftrious character of the natives appears in the cultivated ftate of their mountains, many parts of which prefent the face of a fine garden. Springs, judicioufly directed, water their mulberry plantations, in

P 2 which

which confift the wealth of the country; and fuch is the fuperior quality and high value of the filk raifed from the mulberry-leaves, that the farmer obtains by his trees, at little expence and labour, a competent fubfiftence for his family. Wine, oil, and figs, are articles from which he likewife derives confiderable emolument.

We do not meet here with any thing to compare with the riches and luxury of European nations; but as the fortunes of individuals are lefs unequal, poverty and indigence, which confume the loweft clafs of the people in the fineft provinces of France, are altogether unknown.

Should any perfon be defirous to know where man is fubjected to the leaft penury and wretchednefs, I would refer him to the mountains of Syria, where the refinements of luxury are indeed precluded, but where he would amply enjoy every thing neceflary to his peace and happinefs. There the powers of the mind are not chilled and exafperated by the feverities of an inhofpitable climate, neither are they debafed and enervated by the fecure pofleflion of unfolicited

cited abundance. Subsistence, though easy, is not, however, to be obtained without bodily labour, which only tends, however, to brace the nerves and strengthen the limbs. The avocations of the people are entertaining to the mind, at the same time that they are beneficial to the body, and divert them from any thirst after gratifications which are only necessary to the happiness of those devoted to habits of idleness and intemperance. He who were to look forward to a state of vacancy and idleness, as the period when he should begin to enjoy life, would, were he ever to attain it, probably find himself miserably disappointed. Moderate labour, and a temperate diet, rendering the body healthy and robust, impart also vigour to the mind; and hence arises that fine relish for those innocent pleasures which delight the industrious man after fatigue, a higher gratification than is ever experienced by his wealthier, but more indolent neighbour.

Nocte fatigatum somnus, non cura puellæ,
Excepit; et pingui membra quiete levat.

In vain would the traveller expect to meet, in thefe mountains, with men of great learning, or of very polifhed and refined manners; but he will find men in their beft and happieft ftate, men purfuing their duty from the impulfe of natural fentiment; firm friends, good fathers, virtuous citizens: and fuch characters are of more benefit to the world than the rich, idle, and luxurious, who in more refined countries contaminate the manners of the people by their example, without contributing in any degree to the real interefts of mankind.

The monks of Syria are neither profound theologians, nor extremely rigid in their manners. The rules of their orders are fimple, and fcrupuloufly obferved; and they are in reality what they affect to be in appearance, humble fervants and difciples of their Mafter, earning their daily bread by honeft labour, and the induftry of their hands.

The fecular clergy have little either of learning or rank to diftinguifh them from the vulgar; but though their knowledge is chiefly confined to the New Teftament, they

they are men of regular and pious lives, and highly efteemed by their flocks. Little indebted to the emoluments of a liberal public eftablifhment, they earn by toil, and the fweat of their brows, a fubfiftence for their wives and children. They give conftant attendance to the fervice of the altar, preach the gofpel to the poor, and enforce Chriftian morality by their example, to which the abolition of celibacy among them has been an advantage. The attention they beftow on the education of their own families furnifhes an important leffon to thofe who are lefs immediately under their eye. I have always confidered marriage as a natural duty, and conftituting one of the inalienable rights of mankind.

The laws and maxims of policy which prevail in the countries that were firft peopled, appear to me, in general, to be the beft; but no laws or inftitutions, how wifely foever fuggefted, are able to reftrain the defires of men affembled in great cities: in the country alone the traveller may hope to difcover their original meaning and intention. There the peafant, removed from the depraved fociety of the citizen, from the improper difpofal of his time, and every means of corruption, implicitly follows the laws and cuftoms of his anceftors.

It is a maxim with eaftern nations, that a man fhall be bound by the obligations of marriage, without any previous acquaintance with his intended wife. Now, few inftitutions can immediately appear more whimfical and abfurd. In experience, however, the inconveniencies we might think incident to fuch a practice are not felt; and I am fatisfied, from all I have obferved in the families of the mountaineers, amongft whom I made it my bufinefs to refide, that the feuds and animofities of domeftic life are much lefs frequent there than in the countries of Europe. It is likewife ufual in India to marry at the age of eight or ten, and a girl is generally betrothed to a particular hufband at the age of three or four; and I repeat, that in my experience I had the good fortune never to meet with a fingle couple who feemed to have been injudicioufly ciously or unhappily paired. Educated together from the years of childhood, they become familiar with each other's humour, acquire the character of situation, and are not likely to experience in advanced life any thing that can reasonably give occasion to surprize. The husband exercises dominion over his companion, while she uses with success, in her turn, her natural weapons of tears, gentleness, and submission. Thus, between a couple of Asiatics, born, as it should seem, with a kind of innate rectitude of mind, we naturally expect the most happy and cordial union. Respecting the liberty of free choice, in which the strength of the argument on our side seems to consist, I am afraid that in the tender and inexperienced mind there frequently springs from this very source a love of variety; for the woman who conceives herself entitled to chuse in one instance, may see little harm in exercising the same right a second time, provided she happens to meet with another person whose character is better fitted to engage her affections.

CHAP.

CHAP. XXIV.

Singular opinions of the Asiatics respecting the sexes, and the commerce which should be maintained betwixt them.—Abject state of the females in the nations of the east.—Diversions and pursuits of the Syrian women.—Tenacity of the natives of Syria in preserving their ancient customs.—Their social distinctions.

IT is an opinion pretty generally received among the nations of Asia, that the morals of the women have a strong influence on society at large, as well as on their own children. But they have an idea, perhaps a little more peculiar to themselves, to wit, that the quality and intensity of sentiment in the male sex result partly from the allurements of pleasure, partly from prejudice and habit, and partly from the dread of those evils which tend to the destruction of the individual. Desire, hope, love, hatred, and,

and, in general, all our fentiments and actions, depend, according to them, upon a felfifh principle of fear, which, in proportion as we are imprefied with the danger of defeat, or the hope of victory, produces weaknefs or courage.

But of fuch as confider fear or an interefted concern for our own welfare, as the ultimate principle of human fentiment and conduct, I would afk, Whether a mother's fondnefs for her child, as the Afiatics feem to believe, contains no ingredient of a more liberal origin than that fweet fenfation of pleafure fhe experiences at the end of her labour, when fhe reflects that her fufferings were occafioned by a being which makes a part of herfelf, and therefore entitled to her kindeft affections? Muft the gradual increafe of paternal affection be referred folely to habit, and the attachment one neceffarily acquires for an object which cofts fo much care and anxiety? In the fame manner is the fentiment of friendfhip, a fentiment equally rare and valuable, to be refolved into habit, or the hope of deriving advantage from our friend? Are pity, charity,

rity, and beneficence, which are excited by the misfortunes of others, of no higher account than that of a mean reflex fentiment on our own condition? In a word, are magnanimity, generofity, and courage, nothing better than different modifications of the fame interefted principle, congratulating itfelf on having efcaped thofe evils which we wifh to alleviate in others?—This fyftem is too humiliating to the human fpecies to be founded in nature.

In Arabia, and in all the countries with which the Arabs have an intercourfe, the women are fubjected to the veil, and almoft entirely fecluded from the company of the men. Each fex lives apart, and in conformity to their own humours; infomuch that the hufband paffes but a fmall part of his time with his wife. This cuftom is confidered as extremely beneficial to both parties; for, as the object of marriage is mutual fidelity, the great danger incident to happinefs in that ftate is to be apprehended from an eafy and frequent communication between the fexes: and as the temper and difpofitions of a man and his wife do not at

all

all times coalefce, the feldomer they meet the fewer occafions will occur of domeftic ftrife and animofity. Hence they conclude that nothing can be expected from an unreftrained intercourfe betwixt the fexes, but exceffes of paffion in the one, danger to the innocence of the other, and multiplied caufes of contention in both. Accordingly, the only perfons of different fexes who enjoy any fhare of focial intercourfe, are fuch as ftand in the neareft degrees of confanguinity; a pleafure, however, which is permitted even to them fparingly and on rare occafions. In many families thefe maxims of referve are fo ftrictly obferved, that as foon as boys attain the years of thirteen or fourteen, they are removed to a particular wing of the building, named Manfoul, which is entirely unconnected with the female apartments.

Men in eaftern nations are extremely jealous of their fuperiority over the female fex; and hence it is that a man feldom condefcends to eat with his wife. It is her bufinefs to ferve her hufband at table with all the care and affiduity of a fervant; nor does

does fhe find herfelf at liberty to fit down to her meal until he has concluded his. He never defires her opinion, or deigns to converfe with her on the fubject of family affairs. He feldom affigns her a tafk that may not be performed without ftirring abroad, or any bufinefs abroad but what may be performed with her veil. Women in every condition of life are fubjected to thefe regulations, and their time is all employed with their children and in houfehold affairs, which, however, from their plain and fimple manners, require little application. My feelings revolted againft this flavifh and fubordinate condition of the fex. But I was ftruck with the great fimilarity I difcovered in this point between the manners of the American favages and thofe of the Arabs, as well as other Afiatic tribes; a refemblance extremely furprifing, when we confider the great diftance the Arab and American are removed from each other. In America the favage charges himfelf with nothing but his gun, while his wife follows, loaded with every article of the family baggage. In

Afia

Afia it is the fame: the favage entertains no converfation whatever with his wife; nor does fhe prefume to be prefent at any of his parties. The fame are the manners of Syria, and indeed of the Afiatic continent in general. In the Biffayan ifles, and among the Marratta tribes, as well as in America, the fields of Indian corn are cultivated by the women alone. The Arab mounts his afs, and leaves his wife, with a large bundle on her head, to follow him on foot. The favage fits at his eafe in his canoe, while his wife keeps tugging at the oar without murmur or complaint. Now it appears very remarkable that two people inhabiting oppofite hemifpheres of the globe, the one ancient and the other probably modern, fhould fo ftrongly refemble each other; whilft Europeans, at an equal diftance from both, have manners entirely different.

In Arabia, a numerous family is an object of great defire to both fexes. Hence an old maiden, an aged batchelor, and a barren woman, are regarded with a fentiment bordering on contempt. The hufband

band and wife are equally delighted at the birth of a child; and upon the delivery of the firſt male, reſign their own name, in order to take the more honourable appellation of the child's parents. Thus, ſhould Peter and Mary have a ſon, James, they immediately ceaſe to be Peter and Mary, and are ſtyled henceforth the father and mother of James. The father of James begins to cultivate his beard, as a badge of his newly acquired dignity, as well as to attract that reſpect and veneration which he conceives now due to him from the public. Of this deſcription, among others, are the Syrian Arabs. The Arabs of the Bedouin tribes aſſume the name of the common ſtock : hence Ben Halet, or the children of Halet. A title, I conceive, by which all the individuals of the tribe are repreſented as brethren, and which is at the ſame time intereſting to the mind, and extremely uſeful in ſociety. It very ſenſibly implies a reciprocal obligation; in one view admoniſhing the children of the duty and reſpect they owe to their fathers; in another, engaging the parent to maintain a kind and
affectionate

affectionate behaviour towards children whofe names it is his glory to bear.

From the extreme referve maintained between the fexes, we are not to expect in the circles of Syria that gaiety of manners, or highly feafoned though fuperficial converfation, to which, in different countries of Europe, a conftant and anxious defire of pleafing the women have given occafion. The youth, in the moft lively period of life, are all equally ferious in their deportment and converfation; fupporting a fobriety of manners which gradually increafes as they advance in years. They fpeak little, and never lofe fight of the object they had firft in view. A total want of vivacity, the habit of fmoking, which gives occafion to frequent paufes, and that of ftroking their beards and handling a kind of chaplet, allow them time to confider and digeft their queftions and replies. In converfation they are fhort and energetic, proportioning the number of their words to the nature of the fubject; hence a peculiar characteriftic of their language, which, if I may prefume to form an opinion on

Vol. II.   Q   the

the little knowledge I was able to acquire of it during my abode in this country, is the moſt ſimple and expreſſive in the world.

The fair ſex are never introduced as a topic of converſation; nay, they even paſs in the ſtreets without obtaining the ſmalleſt notice from the men. The places they are known to frequent are deemed ſacred and inacceſſible; and a man would feel himſelf affronted, who ſhould be accuſed of having remarked or ſaluted a woman in public. Europeans, I know, conſider theſe eaſtern manners as the reſult of gloomy jealouſy; but I rather regard them as the conſequences of a punctilious delicacy relative to the point of honour in the ſex, who, according to the maxims of Aſia, are not ſuppoſed to have any acquaintance with men, except in the perſon of one individual. The women, neverthelefs, contrive to paſs the time agreeably by themſelves; and as the ſole object of their parties is amuſement, little affected by any ingredient that can give occaſion to latent difguſt, they probably experience more real gaiety

gaiety of heart than the fair European, who, in the midst of her crowded and promiscuous assemblies, is often liable to be disturbed by envy, jealousy, and resentment. With a mind easy and unembarrassed, the Asiatic seems to move in a sphere which affords a finer relish for the society and enjoyment of her companions. She receives the visits of her friends in her own apartments, while the garden, the bath, and the tomb, are the places of her public resort. This Oriental custom of frequenting the tombs, is a strong proof of female sensibility; the mind being nicely susceptible of impressions, but at the same time endowed with a peculiar versatility of reflection, has stamped its own image on this kind of assembly. Upon their arrival at the grave of a deceased friend, they give full vent to the sorrow and anguish of their bosoms; afterwards they gradually enter into conversation, which takes a serious, gay, or even ludicrous turn, according to their different characters. After all, a good heart may here find relief; and many, I have no doubt, profit by the leſſons of moral inſtruction they receive at the grave, however extraordinary the cuſtom itſelf may appear to ſtrangers.

The natives of this country are extremely tenacious of ancient cuſtoms; a circumſtance which will account for the many veſtiges we ſtill trace of the manners and uſages of the ancient patriarchs. The *tanour*, or cylindrical oven, employed in baking their cakes, and the *tantoura*, or ſilver cone, a kind of head-dreſs worn by the women among the Druſes, are evidently the ſame with the Jewiſh oven and Judith's mitre. The manners of Abraham and his family may be traced in the habits and purſuits of the Bedouin ſhepherds, who, ſince the age of Laban, have led about their flocks during the day, and folded them in the evening. The ſtyle of the Arabic language in our own times is the ſame with that of the Old Teſtament, a ſameneſs which could only have been preſerved by an anxious attachment to the modes and cuſtoms of their progenitors.

Being originally deſcended from wandering tribes, they are at little pains to adorn their

their houses; and the different articles of their furniture are so contrived as to be easily packed up for the convenience of travelling. Riding is of all exercises that of which they are most passionately fond. In their persons they are clean, sober and simple in their manners, and entire strangers to luxury. The pompous and arrogant genius of the Turk has been communicated in no degree to the inhabitants of this country, whose courage and virtuous simplicity have hitherto bid defiance to the fetters of a despotic master. They are, however, selfish, and sometimes, though rarely, fraudulent towards the French, who, they insist, ought to pay them a certain tribute in consideration of that commerce they are permitted to carry on in their harbours. The extreme difference they, besides, discover between the manners of France and those of Syria, disposes them to look down on the natives of the former country with disdain.

In Syria we find four orders of men only: first, princes; secondly, lords and governors;

governors; thirdly, opulent merchants and farmers; and laftly, the poorer peafantry, and all below them. A prince or lord, provided he abftains from commerce, may defcend from his rank in order to redeem his decayed fortune, without lofing one tittle of the refpect due to his birth. The merchant and farmer, how opulent foever their circumftances, are incapable of rifing to a higher order, but, like the prince, and for fimilar reafons, may defcend to a lower condition without any diminution of their confequence; and in many inftances the children of reduced governors, clergymen, and merchants, are not afhamed to enter into the fervice of ftrangers, who are greatly their inferiors in point of birth. The right every individual poffeffes of redreffing his own wrongs has given occafion to fomething fimilar to our point of honour, which prevails equally among all orders of men. The Arab retaliates on his adverfary, how eminent foever his rank, the moment he receives an affront; a cuftom which,

which, confidering the circumftances of the country, more effectually reftrains violence than the operation of the fevereft laws for the punifhment of crimes. If the Arab fhews a conftant deference towards the perfon of his chief, it is on account of qualities really ufeful to the tribe; but as in all ranks, manners, drefs, and the fare of the table, are extremely fimilar, it is difficult on ordinary occafions to diftinguifh one order of men from another. Every one is acquainted with the high pedigree of an Arabian chieftain, who, neverthelefs, in his affability and condefcenfion to his inferiors, forms a ftriking contraft to the upftart nobility of modern nations. The prince, the lord, and the peafant, fit down to the fame table, enter familiarly into converfation, and light their pipes at the fame taper, under as little ceremony and conftraint as we expect to meet with in the fociety of brothers. Laftly, men in all conditions of life eat, fleep, and work together; infomuch that I have often miftaken a lord for a peafant, and a peafant for a prince: the fuperior beauty of his horfe, and the brightnefs of his armour, being the only marks by which the latter may be known.

CHAP. XXV.

The Author returns to the Syrian Mountains.—The village of Abey and its environs defcribed.—Ceremonies obferved at a Drufan funeral.—Paftoral mode of life of the Drufes.—Refidence in the town of Dair-el-Kamar.

WISHING to become better acquainted with the natives of the Syrian mountains, I propofed to give them a little more of my time, and particularly to vifit the people called Drufes; meanwhile I refolved to pay my refpects once more to my friends the Maronites of Quefrouan, and accordingly my firft ftage was to Aïntoura. From thence I continued my journey towards Agoufta, where I hoped

to

to have had the honour of meeting with the patriarch of Antioch. At Aintoura I faluted my friend the fuperior of the jefuits, who earneftly requefted me to pafs fome time at the convent; but I excufed myfelf, and went to fleep at Baruth.

Next day, having fet out for a place named Abey, fituated among the Drufes, I croffed the plain of Baruth diagonally, and travelled three leagues fouthward. In the vicinity of the town this plain is planted with mulberry-trees. I came foon after to a beautiful foreft of pines in a quincunxial form, clofe to a little Arabian encampment. Paffing a dry defart foil with fome olive-trees, and a few plantations of the mulberry-tree, I arrived at a large village named Chouifah, near the foot of a mountain, the refidence and patrimonial inheritance of an obfcure emir. Keeping this village on the left, I afcended by a long and 'fteep path, and paffed another large village on the right. Here the traveller croffes feveral mountains, and having afcended to a confiderable height, finds a large village named Aramon, containing
a caftle

a caftle or feraglio, which belongs to the family of the reigning emir. The adjacent country appears to be well watered, and is planted with olive and mulberry-trees. Having defcended from Aramon, and croffed other mountains, with their intervening vallies, I at length difcovered, from the top of a high ridge, the village of Abey ftanding on an eminence before me. I paffed a little village, from whofe emir I received every attention, and arrived at Abey in the evening, after a journey of feven leagues.

This village was once the refidence of an emir's family, which is now entirely extinct. It is fituated at the diftance of two leagues from a large town named Dair-el-Kamar, which is the capital of the Drufan country, and the feat of the grand Emir and his relations. Its pofition, at three leagues diftance from the fea, and one from the river Thamour, is by far the fineft I have yet met with. Abey is built on the third flight of a vaft amphitheatre, formed by three mountains piled one above another, and occupying the whole intervening

ing space between the village and the Mediterranean. From this lofty ridge the eye commands a view of Sidon and Baruth, with their adjacent plains. The descent to the second flight is formed by a small ridge or Afs's Back, on each side of which is a little valley at the bottom of a very high and steep precipice: both vallies are watered by a copious rivulet of fine water, supplied by the springs in the neighbourhood of Abey. These springs are of great use in watering the sides of the mountains, which, notwithstanding their very abrupt descent, are dressed in an amphitheatrical form, and planted with the mulberry-tree. There are likewise five or six other springs in this district, on the confines of which the traveller finds square plantations of the walnut-tree.

I fixed my head quarters in a Capuchin convent, from the superior of which I met with kindness and hospitality. This convent overlooks five or six highland villages, in which I spent the greater part of my time; and as the principal object of this excursion was to observe the manners of a

people

people hitherto but little known, I omitted nothing that could introduce me to their acquaintance and good graces. Besides living with them, I aſſiſted at all their ruſtic diverſions, and even made myſelf uſeful by herding their ſheep and goats; and I have the ſatisfaction to think that I was the cauſe of diminiſhing, in ſome degree, that averſion which, contrary to their known hoſpitality, and the regard they profeſs to entertain for ſtrangers, they had retained againſt the French. After conforming to the life of a ſavage in America, a Bramin in India, and an Arab in the deſert, I was now a ſhepherd on the mountains of the Druſes; and often have I admired the inſtinct of my goats, who, after bleating and ſtamping with their feet, as if in defiance of the precipice that ſeparated them from the flock, bounded with alacrity to the oppoſite cliff. The extraordinary aſpect of the rocky ridges, which in the courſe of my paſtoral employment I had frequently occaſion to obſerve, as well as the ſocial and friendly intercourſe of my fellow-ſhepherds, were the grateful wages

of

of many painful and difficult excursions over the distant hills.

During my abode in this country I assisted at several funerals, Drusan as well as Christian; ceremonies which, with a little difference in the form of their prayers, are in other respects extremely similar. In a few hours after he expires, the deceased is laid out under a tent, dressed in his ordinary apparel and warlike accoutrements; and the more devout Druses, concerning whom it is my intention to speak, place likewise a pious book in his hands. The women hasten from all quarters, in order to seat themselves around the corpse, and to bedew it with their tears; while the men, after making the vallies to resound with the most dismal cries and lamentations, as a signal to the adjacent villages of the event that has happened, remain in deep silence at a small distance from the tent. In a little time the friends of the deceased come flocking from their respective villages; and as soon as they are perceived at the tent, the nearest relations take up the body, and set off to meet them. Having joined their acquaintances,

acquaintances, they carry the corpfe (but at fome diftance from the houfes) round the village, expreffing the moft clamorous regret by cries and groans, waving their handkerchiefs in the air, and gefticulating with their bodies in a violent manner. The corpfe is now returned to the tent, where the women refume their former fituation, repeating, however, their part of the ceremony at every new arrival of friends. Thus the dead body lies in a kind of ftate till next morning, when the inhabitants of the village, Chriftians as well as Drufes, affemble, and having laid it on a bier, carry it out before the door in profound filence. Here a Catholic or Drufan prieft, according to the religion of the defunct, begins the fervice, which confifts of a number of prayers, recited in a low tone of voice. The preparations for the departure of the bier are accompanied with the moft doleful howling and even refiftance of the women, who feem unable to brook a final feparation. Meanwhile the men continue with mournful gravity as paffive fpectators. At length the principal mourners retire weeping and
inconfolable

inconfolable into the houfe, when it is the bufinefs of the men to conduct the deceafed to his grave. When the funeral is over, the ftrangers are invited by the inhabitants of the village to their feveral houfes, where, while they commemorate the virtues of the dead, they entertain their guefts in the beft manner they are able.

I now paid a vifit to the town of Dair-el-Kamar, fituated near the banks of the Thamour, and on the fide of a mountain oppofite to that on which ftands the village of Abey. I paffed the river by a bridge built partly over a cruft of petrified clay, which prefents to the view of the traveller rocks that had been immerfed in the mud, and tracks occafioned by runs of water previoufly to the period of its petrifaction. El-Kamar is well fupplied with excellent water, and ftands at leaft equally high with the village of Abey, but is more difficult of accefs. The palaces or feraglios, which belong to the emirs of the reigning family, are fine buildings; the churches are handfome,

fome, and built in good tafte; and the houfes of fome cheiks and commandants have large and convenient apartments; but the reft of the town confifts of mean and ill-conftructed habitations. The Drufes do not exceed one half of the inhabitants, while the remainder are all Maronites and Greek Catholics; for, owing to the zeal and induftry of the Capuchin miflionaries, who in the courfe of twenty years have reftored to the communion of the Romifh church nearly three-fourths of the nation, there are at prefent only a very few fchifmatic Greeks in thefe parts.

CHAP. XXVI.

Government and political regulations of the Land of Souf.—Sagacity of the grand emir of Turkey in dividing the interests of the cheiks or governors.—State of warfare betwixt the different tribes.—Their inveterate hatred to strangers.—Regulations of internal policy.

THE mountains south of the river Thamour are named the Land of Souf, though Dair-el-Kamar is in this district, and the ordinary residence of the emirs. As many of the emirs, however, have removed to Baruth, they are by no means so powerful, or of so much consequence here, as upon the northern parts of the river. A great cheik in the country of Souf frequently eludes the homage which he owes to the authority of the grand emir. The third and last division of the mountains is inhabited by cheiks of tolerably regular and quiet manners, as well as by two families of emirs, who are proprietors of a very confiderable territory. The Chriftian cheiks, or the defcendants of the houfe of Gazen, who are the great lords of Quefrouan, though pofleffed of a large and populous country, give little interruption to the emir's government. The fact feems to be, that the cheiks being extremely numerous, but broken into fmall branches, are incapable of uniting in one body, and confequently of forming or executing any premeditated plan of oppofition to his authority; a circumftance, the advantages accruing from which to his tranquillity have not efcaped the fagacity of the grand emir, who, by fowing diffention and jealoufy among their different members, is enabled to preferve the balance of power in his own hands, and to prevent the cheiks entering into any dangerous combination againft him.

The forms of legal procedure within thefe mountains are extremely fimple. The cheik adminifters juftice to the inhabitants of his own village; but in terminating

nating their suits, particularly those of a civil nature, he acts for the greater part as an arbiter or umpire between the parties. If the persons concerned either decline his jurisdiction, or refuse to acquiesce in his decree, he may appeal to the court of the grand emir, who, except in actions of property situated in Quefrouan, and holding of the house of Gazen, or belonging to inferior emirs possessing an exclusive jurisdiction over their own estates, is the ultimate and supreme judge. The administration of justice, owing to the weak state of civil authority, is by no means severe; and hence the judge seldom attempts to execute a more rigorous sentence than that of quartering troops on the delinquent, or burning his mulberry-plantations. The apprehension of offenders is attended with such danger and difficulty, as to render the infliction of corporal punishment extremely rare. A mountaineer is never seen without the walls of his cottage unprovided with a dagger or sabre; and if he proposes to go to any considerable distance from home, he is armed likewise with a gun

gun and piftols. By the maxims of a law which cuftom has eftablifhed, a man is warranted to repel force by force, and to redrefs his own wrongs in the beft manner he can ; and therefore whoever conceives himfelf infulted, difpatches his antagonift the moment he finds an opportunity of levelling his piece at him, with as little concern as he would kill a woodcock.

A man who gives his daughter in marriage to any but one of his own relations is confidered as bringing reproach on himfelf and his tribe: and I have been told that fuch as have ventured to tranfgrefs this rule of family alliance have been difpatched by the dagger, before the confummation of the nuptials. Families of the fame blood entertain the moft clannifh attachment, infomuch that whoever offers an injury or affront to one, is held to be in a ftate of hoftility with the whole tribe. In a criminal accufation, befides the protection derived to the offender from the combined force of his own kindred, if he dreads an obftinate profecution on the part of the family offended, or at the inftance of the

grand

grand emir, and is apprehenfive that all the power of his friends will be unable to avail him, he retires under the protection of fome cheik or inferior emir, who, in order to avoid the infamy he would incur by violating the rules of hofpitality, fhelters him from the purfuit of his enemies.

The emirs and cheiks who are not related to the reigning family, are not entitled to take into their fervice and pay, any but the vaffals and retainers on their own eftates. But whoever is defcended from the family of the grand emir may make levies all over the mountains ; a circumftance which tends greatly to circumfcribe the emir's authority whenever a difpute happens between him and any of his relations. Meanwhile it is the policy and conftant bufinefs of the Bafha to create and foment fuch diffentions, no lefs with a view to weaken the authority of the emir's government, than, by becoming at laft the umpire of their quarrels, to afford himfelf an opportunity of extorting prefents from both parties. The differences which occafionally arife between the emirs and
cheiks

cheiks are never of equally ferious confequences with thofe between individual families. The recruits which both parties bring
into the field confift of men who have no
ftronger motive to action than their own ca-
price, or the ties of acquaintance, to prefer
the pay of one emir or cheik to that of
another. As branches of the fame family
are fometimes fcattered in feparate villages,
and fubject to different chiefs, it frequently happens that the father and fon find
themfelves oppofed to each other. The two
armies, however, thus compofed, are always fufficiently careful not to fhed the
blood of their friends, out of compliment
to their leaders. The chief mifchief to be
apprehended in fuch fituations, is a great
deal of clamour, riot, and confufion. As
foon as the armies are in prefence of each
other, the cheiks and heads of the peafantry deliver their fentiments upon the
matter; and as every one thinks himfelf
entitled to a fhare in the adminiftration of
affairs, the troops in general canvafs the
grounds of the difpute in their turn. If
the popular opinion happens to be in favour

vour of a pacification, it is intimated by the cheiks to the commanders in chief, who commonly find it expedient to accede to the terms dictated by their retainers. But ſhould the terms of accommodation, infiſted upon by the parties, be fo widely different as to preclude all hopes of accommodation, the congrefs breaks up, and after committing fome devaſtation on the enemy's mulberry-plantations, every man returns to his own houfe, fatisfied with what he has performed. The peafant, therefore, befides having had an opportunity of difplaying his military talents, pockets the pay of the emir for his fervices, and returns to his plough, the only perfon benefited by the campaign.

But if their inteſtine quarrels are tame and inoffenfive, the wars they wage againſt ſtrangers are proportionally fanguinary and fierce; and hence that terror with which they are regarded by all around them. Various inſtances render the fact undoubted, that a mountaineer undertakes aſſaſſination at the command of the emir, and frequently goes alone, and in cold blood, to execute

his

his purpofe on the devoted victim, whether in the city or the camp. A Drufan fome time fince ftabbed the Aga of the cuftoms at Sidon, in the prefence of his clerks, whilft the friend of the affaffin, a Maronite, ftood at the gate of the town with a piftol in one hand and a fabre in the other, in order to cover the murderer's retreat.

The money or tribute payable to the Grand Signior is levied by the emir from the cheiks, who apportion it in their turn on their refpective villages, and collect it from individuals by a fair affeffment. But in fuch villages as hold directly of the grand emir, this tax is impofed by a rate fixed in an affembly of the inhabitants. It is competent to thefe affemblies to deliberate and decide on all bufinefs of national concern, fuch as public repairs, and the beft methods of improving and cultivating the foil. The taxes are inconfiderable, and impofed with ftrict impartiality, according to every man's property in land or cattle. The wealth of the people at large confifts chiefly in goats, which occafion no expence, and but little attention; for fuch is the genial

nial warmth of this climate, that at one degree of elevation, or another, in thefe regions, the inhabitants are affured of fine pafture at all feafons of the year.

CHAP. XXVII.

Various particulars refpecting the cuftoms and religious tenets of the inhabitants of the land of Souf.—The Author returns to Baruth, and afterwards vifits Mafra and feveral other villages in the province of Quefrouan. Comparifon betwixt the manners and principles of the Greeks and Arabs.

ONE half of the inhabitants in the land of Souf are Chriftians; a third are Catholic Greeks; and the reft Maronites. The fchifmatic Greeks are fo inconfiderable in number as to be of little confequence. In the other diftricts of thefe mountains one half of the people are of the fect of Maronites, with very few either of fchifmatic or Catholic Greeks; the other half are

are compofed of Drufes, divided into two claffes: the firft have no other religion than that of nature; while the fecond, named Acquelle or fpiritual Drufes, are the votaries of a religion, the principles of which are altogether unknown. The honour of belonging to this clafs is not to be attained by birth, but by a life of fimplicity, innocence, and religious penitence. Its votaries appear dreffed in black, or in a ftriped garment black and white, wear a white turban, but of a modeft form, and are not allowed, by the rules of their order, to carry arms, except when all the cheiks take the field, or in cafes of the greateft emergency. Dreading to become acceffaries to the guilt of thofe who may have acquired property by unjuft or unfair means, they never eat with, nor will receive a prefent, but from men of the moft irreproachable characters. Much of their time is fpent in reading the five books of Mofes, which in Arabic are named Taura, and at ftated times they affemble to pray in their oratories; but what thefe oratories contain I neither had an opportunity of examining myfelf, nor of learning

ing from others. On the days allotted to prayer and the services of the oratory, they keep watch upon the neighbouring hills to the distance of half a league all around. In houses, named *caloué*, situated on the tops of the most steep and inacceffible rocks, and in the vicinity of their villages, the most devout of this order shut themselves up for several weeks together. Some, I was affured, admit penitents to auricular confeffion, whose fins urge them to seek confolation in the exercise of this Christian privilege. The memory of those Acquelle who die, as they exprefs it, in the sweet odours of holinefs, is held in the deepeft veneration, while their bodies have the honour to be depofited in the little oratory. They practice great austerities, fafting, prayer, and an entire abstinence from every species of pleafure. One example I had occafion to obferve in a spiritual at Abey, who fubfifted on bread and water alone. In this village is the body of an ancient Drufan, an object of great veneration over the whole country. The Acquelle enter our churches with a modeft, collected, and refpectful deportment, and in

this

this particular fet an example to all Chriftians; though it muft be allowed that the Chriftians of thefe parts have a much more devout behaviour at divine worfhip than is always to be met with in Europe. In fine, many of the Acquelle feem to attend with fatisfaction to the truths of the gofpel; but the fear of ridicule, and the forfeiture of their goods, prefent great difficulties to their converfion. Hence the reafon why the labours of our Capuchin miffionaries, who, by their zeal, the purity of their manners, and particularly their fkill in the practice of medicine, are highly refpected in this country, have been of fo little avail. The purity and piety of their lives, however, procuring them accefs to the firft families, feveral of the emirs' wives have been converted to the Chriftian faith. The converfion of the mothers has led to the baptifm of fome of their children, with the confent of the emir himfelf, who from his high rank is in a condition to defpife the cenfure and reproach of his neighbours. I have fome reafon to believe that there are emirs who would have little objection to be baptifed themfelves, provided the

the court of Rome, in confideration of inward conformity, would difpenfe with their obfervance of the external rites of the church.

The other clafs of Drufes is extremely rude and uninformed; and though fome of them are faid to worfhip the true God, they may be confidered in general as having no fixed religious opinions whatever. I am told they fometimes read the Taura, or books of Mofes; but I can only fay, from my own obfervation, that in their perfons and deportment they are much more barbarous and uncultivated than either the Chriftians or their more pious brethren the Acquelle. Among thefe Drufes, however, I have known men of very good character. They value themfelves highly on their perfonal courage; and I am not fure that my bad opinion of their morals may not proceed from prejudice and their outward appearance.

That very extenfive valley ftretching in length from Sidon to the river Ibrahim, in breadth from the fea to Beca, and fituated between the mountains of the Drufes and thofe those of Damascus, properly named Anti-Libanus, is wholly under the dominion of the grand emir. The tribes inhabiting the country between Sidon and the river Thamour are brave, well made in their persons, and confiderably civilized. From the Thamour all the way to the province of Quefrouan the character of the people is more rude and ferocious. The natives of Quefrouan are lefs arrogant, but impatient of ftrangers, and addicted to revenge. Laftly, in the country above Quefrouan, known by the name of Anti-Quefrouan, the manners of the people are ftill more coarfe and favage; and thus I was able to diftinguifh four different fhades of character in the natives of thefe mountains. Except, however, in certain peculiarities, the manners of the country in general are very much the fame. Although a ftranger, I lived in their villages without the leaft apprehenfion either of robbery or affaffination; and, during the three months I paffed at Abey, flept in a garden near the great road, without wall or fence of any kind, and without meeting with the fmalleft difturbance.

I had

I had eafy accefs to the fociety of twelve villages in the neighbourhood. Near that of Roche-maya I was fhewn the enormous fragment of a mountain, which, undermined, in procefs of time had rolled down into a valley watered by the Thamour. A village and feveral little hamlets lay buried under the ruins, and the courfe of the current was for fome time completely interrupted; but the river gradually wafhing away the loofe and earthy parts of the mafs, at length recovered its ufual channel.

I now quitted my abode in this part of the country, in order to make a fecond vifit to Mafra-Cafan de Bian, which, as I had occafion to mention in my firft expedition, is fituated at the foot of the higheft mountain in Quefrouan; I therefore proceeded to Baruth, and after vifiting my acquaintances at Aintoura and Jelton, foon joined my good friend the paftor of Mafra, where, though in the end of June, I found the houfes ftill occupied by the filk-worm, which fupplies the general and moft lucrative object of commerce in thefe regions.

I likewife

I likewife vifited a village named Beca Touta, whofe cheik the preceding year had conducted me to view the infcription of Elfogra : he was very happy to fee me, and under his protection I went to vifit a handfome female convent of Greek Catholics. This building was erected by a rich merchant of Damafcus, who after fmarting long under the yoke of Turkifh fervitude, had retired to pafs the evening of his life in the quiet of thefe mountains. I faw alfo, in a fequeftered corner of the fame diftrict, the eftates of the Befconta emirs, who are efteemed men of great power and confequence.

Having now made a confiderable ftay in this part of Afia, and being inclined to pafs into Europe without lofs of time, I proceeded directly to St. Jean d'Acre, a port much frequented by the trading fhips of Marfeilles.

At Baruth, Sidon, and ftill more at this place, I made acquaintance with families of Greek origin, whofe manners are by no means equally pure with thofe of the Arabs, and whofe minds, formed to all that

delicacy

delicacy, art, and fubtlety difcoverable in the refinement of their language, are far from being agreeable to my fentiments. In exchange for the honeft heart, manly good fenfe, and naïve vivacity of the Arab, though at times a little ferocious in his temper, I could find nothing in them but the ftudied levity of a deceitful and interefted mind. This led me to make a brief comparifon between the different races of untutored men I had had an opportunity of feeing in the courfe of my travels; and having confidered them in their manners, the entire freedom of their fituation, and their peculiar vigour both of mind and body, I am obliged to hefitate between the Arab and American favage: perhaps, however, the principles of action in the former ought to throw the fcale in his favour, in preference to any other defcription of men whatever. The pleafant and dexterous genius of the Biffayan Indians, the fuavity of manners inherent in the natives of India, and that goodnefs of heart common to all thefe fimple people, united to the fuperior excellency of their climate

and

and foil, give them many advantages in my mind over the condition of Europeans, whether confidered with regard to country, climate, or manners.

CHAP. XXVIII.

The Author embarks at St. Jean d'Acre for Marfeilles.—The veffel touches at Limba, a Turkifh port, where fhe is in danger of being detained.—The contempt in which the French, and other European merchants, in the Turkifh ports, are held by the Turks, accounted for.—After touching at Tunis, the Author at length reaches Marfeilles.

SETTING fail for Marfeilles in the end of June 1771, we bore away for the ifland of Cyprus; which having coafted with a wefterly, and confequently a contrary wind, prevalent in thofe parts during the fummer months, we ftretched northward in order to catch the breeze from that quarter,

quarter, and accordingly found it on the coaft of Caramania. It is to be obferved, that I had experienced a weft wind ever fince my departure from Surat; a wind which blows generally, during the fummer feafon, from the line all the way to the ifland of Candia; generally I fay, for we muft except certain intervals, in which the land breeze prevails. As foon as we came upon the coaft of the gulph of *Satalia*, we faw a fmall veffel, which, getting into our wake, bore down upon us with full fail. We were apprehenfive fhe might prove one of thofe piratical cruizers, which the Ruffian and French armed fhips had driven from the Archipelago into thofe parts; and though we obferved only one man on board, who was at the helm, we fired a fhot; but fhe perfifted in her courfe, and it was not till we had repeated our falute that fhe at laft chofe to fheer off.

As we approached the fouthern coaft of the ifland of Rhodes, finding we were in want of water, we touched at an out-port named Limba from an adjacent village. About half way from the top of a mountain in its vicinity ftand the ruins of two forts, which were anciently built by the knights of Rhodes. We were fupplied with water and frefh provifions from the Grecian villages; but I could not help conftantly comparing the refined Greek with the hardy Arabian; the Greek's cruel fervitude under the Turk, with that highfpirited freedom and independence which cleave to the unpolifhed but manly life of the Arab; the polifhed addrefs, nice food, fmart apparel, and neat apartments of the former, with the coarfe and rude ftate of all thofe articles that fall to the fhare of the latter; and was upon the whole confirmed, that in all focieties of men, a high ftate of civilization and refinement are certain prefages of approaching decline. I obferved with fincere concern how widely thofe two races of men differ from each other in their notions of happinefs, the object of their joint purfuit. The Greek is gay, but felfifh; poor, and yet nice in every thing that relates to the gratification of his appetites. The Arab is lively and generous, equally poor with the Greek; but has few wants

that

that can occasion him a moment's pain or inquietude. What an extreme difference between these two nations! and how badly calculated the one to attain real happiness, compared with the other! The most miserable of the two, however, passes his days amidst all the advantages of an indulgent sky; whilst the other roams the face of a naked desert, which in many respects is unpropitious to the contented enjoyment of life.

Perceiving symptoms of suspicion in the Turks that we had come hither in order to procure provisions for the Russian ships, we made haste to get again under weigh; and, indeed, we had no sooner got clear of the bay, than we observed a vessel near the shore, stealing towards us with little sail. She presently discovered by our motions that she had not escaped our observation, and therefore, setting all her canvas, instantly gave us chace. As we would not betray our apprehensions of danger, we hoisted our flag and pendant; but the enemy, which proved to be a chebec with Turkish colours, probably mistaking us for

a ship

a ſhip of war, when ſhe came a little nearer ſuddenly bore away, a circumſtance which gave us no ſmall ſatisfaction: for, had we been viſited, as a part of our cargo conſiſted of rice, contrary to an ordinance of the Porte, we muſt have been carried back to the iſland of Rhodes, where it is difficult to ſay how long we might have been detained.

I was extremely ſorry to obſerve the very little regard entertained by the Turks for Europeans in general, and particularly for the French. The conſideration of what might have been the iſſue of our being attacked and captured by this chebec naturally led me to theſe reflections; and I brought under review what I had learned from others, as well as what I had obſerved myſelf, reſpecting our commerce and factories in Syria, and other parts of the Levant. I am perſuaded, that beſides the difference of religion and manners ſubſiſting between us and the Aſiatics, which neceſſarily gives occaſion to a mutual eſtrangement, the conduct of the French in thoſe countries contributes ſtill more

to

to lessen our consequence in the estimation of the Turks.

I observed that our merchants in the sea-ports of the Levant are often obliged to hasten their commercial transactions in order to satisfy the demands of their European correspondents;—that they conduct themselves with little method or steadiness in their engagements with the natives, whose uniform accuracy in business forms a striking contrast to the giddiness and levity of the European merchant;—that the Turkish governors, from an extreme intimacy which subsists between them and the merchants, are but too well acquainted with their commercial as well as private affairs, and hence have it in their power to thwart such schemes and speculations of the consul and company as may not coincide with their own views;—that certain favoured houses, named *barataires*, make themselves subservient to the sinister policy of the basha respecting monopolies, practices to which he finds himself invited by the meanness and servility of the merchants; while he is thence emboldened

boldened to refufe their reafonable requefts as often as he may find it expedient. I will not fay that it is always improper in the merchant to make prefents to the governor, or even to affift him with money in cafes of emergency; but I maintain, that the merchant ought to poffefs fuch a degree of fpirit and independence as fhould enable him to refift thofe loans, which are equivalent to extortion, and have no other object than the gratification of official avarice. Good offices, feafonably and frankly beftowed, are no lefs formed to engage the gratitude and efteem of a high-minded people like the Turks, than fervices, originating in fear, and performed in a fneaking and defpicable manner, are fitted to excite their contempt.

The French have a certain number of fhips conftantly employed in the Levant as carriers for the Turkifh merchants. But I am doubtful whether the profits returned by this branch of traffic into the national coffers can be faid to be equivalent to the defertion of our feamen, the corruption of their manners, and

and that lofs of reputation which, by becoming the hirelings of ftrangers, we fuftain as a kingdom, in the eftimation of the Turks. Whatever might be the fentiments of a Dutchman or Ragufan upon a point in which intereft and honour are fo much at variance, I am confident no Englifhman or Spaniard would be inclined to follow our example.

The European conful in the Levant feldom tranfacts bufinefs with the governor but by the mouth of his dragoman, who has often little acquaintance with the language of the country, and is always bàfely fubfervient to the will of the bafha and his fubordinate officers. Hence the requifitions of the conful have little weight; and unlefs methods more perfuafive than the mediation of the dragoman can be devifed, have little chance of being complied with. If an affair of fome delicacy and importance comes to be negociated through the medium of the dragoman, an arrogant bafha, forgetting the refpect due to a great nation, is apt to treat the French, in the perfon of fo humble a reprefentative, with
infolence

infolence and indignity; whereas a man invefted with the commiffion, and a certain part of the fovereign's delegated authority, is a character of a more impofing nature, and would accordingly obtain much more confideration.

We continued our voyage by the channel of Candia; and afterwards, directing our courfe for the coaft of Malta, on the 15th of October came to anchor at that ifland. Here I met with feveral French frigates, on board of which were fome old companions, whofe friendfhip for me was not impaired by my long abfence.

We again put to fea, and after a navigation of fix days, the fhip's owner having bufinefs at Tunis, ftood for that port, where I was kindly received by the French conful. By his means I became acquainted with feveral Mahometans, whofe difpofitions feemed more analogous to the amiable qualities of the Bedouin Arabs of Baffora, and Mafcate, than to the harfh and imperious manners of the Syrian Muffulmen. We got again under fail; but being much retarded by contrary winds,

it

it was not till the 27th of November that we reached the coaſt of Sardinia, where we put in, and remained two days in the gulph of Palma. In this place, ſo near to my native country, I diſcerned with ſincere pleaſure ſome remains of man's natural ſimplicity, which revived all my regret for the honeſt and undepraved manners of our anceſtors.

The firſt perſon who attracted my notice on ſhore, was a man with a long beard, brawny and vigorous, who in thick and ſubſtantial clothing tended a large herd of cattle, as they grazed a piece of marſhy ground on the borders of the road. He was mounted on a beautiful horſe, with a gun ſlung acroſs his ſhoulders. His dwelling was among the neighbouring mountains, where, a ſtranger to refined and degenerate manners, he adhered to the ancient and ſimple uſages of his fathers; and where his own courage and independence of mind had hitherto in ſome meaſure ſet the arms of the conqueror at defiance. The neatneſs and ſimplicity of his dreſs, the firm and manly expreſſion of his eye, and

and the excellent condition of his flocks, as well as the dexterity he difplayed in the management of his horfe and gun, were in my mind powerful arguments for his continuing to defpife the artificial education of the citizen, and to cherifh the ruftic and fimple manners of his native hills.

Having again put to fea, we left the coaft of Sardinia on the weft; paffed at fome diftance from the ifland of Corfica; and after a paffage of feven days, entering the gulph of Marfeilles, landed on the ifle Pomegues, a place deftined for the quarantine of all fuch veffels as arrive from the ports of the Levant. Next day, being the 5th of December 1771, I entered the infirmary of Marfeilles, in order to perform quarantine;—and gave thanks to God, for having conducted me in fafety to the end of my travels.

F I N I S.

www.ingramcontent.com/pod-product-compliance
Lightning Source LLC
Chambersburg PA
CBHW031929230426

43672CB00010B/1861